ASHE Higher Education Report: Volume 33, Number 5
Kelly Ward, Lisa E. Wolf-Wendel, Series Editors

D0825095

Academic Integrity in the Twenty-First Century: A Teaching and Learning Imperative

Tricia Bertram Gallant

Academic Integrity in the Twenty-First Century: A Teaching and Learning
Imperative
Tricia Bertram Gallant
ASHE Higher Education Report: Volume 33, Number 5
Kelly Ward, Lisa E. Wolf-Wendel, Series Editors

ISSN 1551-6970   electronic ISSN 1554-6306   ISBN 978-0-4703-7366-8

The ASHE Higher Education Report is part of the Jossey-Bass Higher and Adult
Education Series and is published six times a year by Wiley Subscription Services,
Inc., A Wiley Company, at Jossey-Bass, 989 Market Street, San Francisco,
California 94103-1741.

For subscription information, see the Back Issue/Subscription Order Form
in the back of this volume.

CALL FOR PROPOSALS: Prospective authors are strongly encouraged to contact
Kelly Ward (kaward@wsu.edu) or Lisa Wolf-Wendel (lwolf@ku.edu). See "About
the ASHE Higher Education Report Series" in the back of this volume.

Visit the Jossey-Bass Web site at **www.josseybass.com.**

Printed in the United States of America on acid-free recycled paper.

The ASHE Higher Education Report is indexed in CIJE: Current Index to Jour-
nals in Education (ERIC), Current Abstracts (EBSCO), Education Index/Abstracts
(H.W. Wilson), ERIC Database (Education Resources Information Center),
Higher Education Abstracts (Claremont Graduate University), IBR & IBZ: Inter-
national Bibliographies of Periodical Literature (K.G. Saur), and Resources in
Education (ERIC).

Advisory Board

The ASHE Higher Education Report Series is sponsored by the Association for the Study of Higher Education (ASHE), which provides an editorial advisory board of ASHE members.

Contents

Executive Summary

Academic integrity, a traditional principle of postsecondary education, has experienced a renaissance after sixteen years of active research and an invigoration of an integrity policy movement in educational institutions across the United States and around the world. Postsecondary education faculty and student affairs professionals have resurrected the principle of academic integrity as a way to respond to perceived increases in cheating and plagiarism by students. Organizational responses have trended toward two dominant strategies—rule compliance and integrity—both rooted in the legacy of the honor code in postsecondary education. The driving question of these strategies ("how do we stop students from cheating?") focuses organizational interventions on students' character and conduct. This focus, however, may have inadvertently restricted the conversation and limited systemic understanding of academic integrity in the contemporary educational institution.

This report broadens the discussion of academic integrity by exploring the history and dimensions of academic misconduct as well as the contemporary forces straining the teaching and learning environment. The results of this exploration suggest that organizational attempts to enhance academic integrity may be more effective if educators shift the driving question from "how can we stop students from cheating?" to "how can we ensure students are learning?" This shift reframes the issue as central to the educational mission of postsecondary institutions and enfolds concerns of student conduct and character into broader concerns about the multiple dimensions of the teaching and learning environment.

Over the last sixteen years, faculty, administrators, and students in universities and colleges around the nation have expressed increasing concerns about ethics and integrity in postsecondary education institutions. Some of these concerns have been targeted at the conduct of administrators, researchers, and faculty. *Addressing Faculty and Student Classroom Improprieties* (Braxton and Bayer, 2004) is one notable example of a rare attempt to address the conduct of faculty and students in the classroom. Other than such few exceptions, the intense focus in research and in practice has been on the conduct of students. Behaviors such as obtaining help from others during exams, using another's words without attribution, and working with others without the permission of the instructor are proliferating and becoming normative among the undergraduate student population. Continued studies by McCabe and others reveal that the number of students self-reporting such behaviors is at par if not slightly increasing from the rates reported in one of the first extensive studies conducted (Bowers, 1964). As a result, student academic misconduct or academic dishonesty has become a substantial area of research and focus of postsecondary education practice.

The principle of academic integrity has been positioned as the prescription for academic misconduct by research and the Center for Academic Integrity (www.academicintegrity.org). According to the center, academic integrity conveys to students that they are expected to be honest, trustworthy, responsible, respectful, and fair by completing work only in ways authorized by the instructor or the institution. This national rhetoric about academic integrity manifests itself locally in institutional documents and organizational structures. The phrase "academic integrity" now routinely appears on institutional Web sites and in student handbooks, academic integrity policies or honor codes are being implemented or revised, and structures to prevent, police, and punish students' academic misconduct are being created.

What has been missing in literature and practice, however, is a thorough consideration of the complexity of the issue and its centrality to the teaching and learning mission of the postsecondary education campus. Dominant contemporary organizational strategies are variations of traditional approaches to controlling students' conduct, approaches tried throughout the history of postsecondary education with yet unproved success. This monograph explores the history of academic misconduct to posit the lessons that can be learned. These lessons suggest overall that academic misconduct is not simply an issue of student character but connected to and shaped by organizational, institutional, and societal contexts. As a result, this monograph suggests a new organizational strategy that enfolds traditional disciplinary and developmental methods into a more robust teaching and learning strategy. Given the moral panic about a "cheating culture" in educational institutions (Callahan, 2004; Maruca, 2005), the in-depth and thorough examination of the issue along with a proposal for a new strategy is timely.

Foreword

Conversations about student development in colleges and universities tend to incorporate rhetoric that addresses learning *and* development. This statement is also true of conversations about teaching that have shifted to encompass teaching *and* learning. The highlight of this shift is to convey the importance of proactive and student-centered environments that view students as actors in teaching, learning, and development processes and not just passive recipients of information.

Tricia Bertram Gallant's monograph, *Academic Integrity in the Twenty-First Century: A Teaching and Learning Imperative,* adopts a proactive and learner-centered orientation. The monograph shifts the focus of academic integrity from that of negative behaviors associated with "misconduct" and "cheating" to integrity as an important part of teaching and learning for all members of the higher education community. Bertram Gallant's intent is not to overlook and address the negative behaviors associated with misconduct but to embed the issue into the teaching and learning process. The monograph does an excellent job of situating the issue of academic integrity in larger historical and societal contexts that compels the reader to think broadly about the topic.

The monograph is sure to be of interest to faculty members committed to the teaching and learning process. The scholarly treatment of the topic of misconduct versus integrity is not only informative but also well written and interesting. Bertram Gallant guides the reader through different historical periods and the manifestations of misconduct during them. This history is not simply a recounting of the "student antics" used to carry out cheating but is instead an insightful and thorough account of the social origins of misconduct. Further, the historical treatment of the topic makes clear that misconduct has been an insidious part of student life for a long time and that the traditional rule compliance and integrity strategies used on campuses for much of this history may be an insufficient response to the issue of misconduct. Bertram Gallant's work pushes faculty members to think in new and creative ways about issues associated with academic misconduct and integrity.

Faculty committed to improving their classroom environments will also find the monograph's focus on teaching and learning to be useful, for it shifts the focus from catching students' academic transgressions to creating classrooms where academic integrity is the norm. The essence of this strategy, according to Bertram Gallant, is reframing the main practical question from "how do we stop students from cheating?" to "how do we ensure students are learning?" Faculty committed to creating improved learning environments are sure to find the monograph useful.

Student affairs practitioners committed to the learning and development of students will also find the monograph useful to help guide their work. A teaching and learning perspective calls for a collaborative effort between student affairs practitioners and faculty members. The teaching and learning orientation requires involvement by all those involved in students' learning and development, not just student affairs personnel, to be actively involved in issues associated with academic integrity. Such a perspective unites student affairs and academic affairs personnel to address issues of misconduct and integrity as part of a larger teaching and learning effort.

Common on many campuses is a process that treats misconduct in the classroom (such as plagiarizing on a paper assignment) similar to the way it would treat out-of-class misconduct (such as underage drinking in residence halls). Students are asked to explain their actions, go through some type of conduct review process involving peers or faculty, given a "verdict" for their actions, and asked to do some type of remediation or, in extreme cases, are expelled from the institution. Although this process has many variations, it tends to be led by student affairs practitioners, with the focus on the actual behavior of student misconduct. A teaching and learning perspective, in contrast, shifts the focus from academic misconduct at the microlevel (the behaviors associated with misconduct) to a macroperspective that recognizes that breaches in academic integrity compromise the teaching and learning process for everyone—faculty, students, and administrators.

The monograph provides useful and concrete examples of how to employ teaching and learning strategies that uphold academic integrity. These examples emanate from different types of institutions. Bertram Gallant challenges readers to think broadly about academic integrity as not just something that is an issue for students. If we as educators want students to behave in ways that uphold standards and ethics of campus life, then faculty and administrators must uphold the same standards. In this way, Bertram Gallant's monograph builds on Braxton and Bayer's *Addressing Faculty and Student Classroom Improprieties* (2004), a volume in the New Directions for Teaching and Learning series published by Jossey-Bass. Bertram Gallant embeds academic integrity in an organizational context that affects and encompasses all members of the campus community.

A teaching and learning environment that ensures that students are learning pushes administrators and faculty members to commit themselves to organizations and environments that are committed to academic integrity at all levels and in all parts of teaching and learning. Bertram Gallant leads the way to make the ideal of academic integrity a reality.

Kelly Ward
Series Editor

Acknowledgments

This book would not have been possible without the work and efforts of hundreds of people before me who have written about or created institutional programs for academic integrity. Their ideas and research have paved the way for the reconsideration presented in this monograph. I thank all of them for their pursuit of academic integrity and their efforts to make educational institutions better places for teaching and learning.

I would specifically like to acknowledge Donald McCabe, whose work has managed to catapult interest in students' academic conduct; the Center for Academic Integrity, whose mission and efforts to raise awareness of academic integrity are admirable; and Patrick Drinan, for introducing me to this topic and being open to new ways of exploring the issue. Thank you also to Kelly Ward, my editor, for working with me on this project and my colleagues at the University of California, San Diego, for stimulating my thinking and informing my practice. And finally, a special acknowledgment to all those in my life who constantly provide support and encouragement, the most important of whom is my husband and best friend, Jamie.

Published online in Wiley InterScience
(www.interscience.wiley.com) • DOI: 10.1002/aehe.3305

Moral Panic: The Contemporary Context of Academic Integrity

THE IMPETUS OF THE CONTEMPORARY academic integrity movement in colleges and universities can perhaps be traced to the 1960s,
when a multi-institutional study declared academic dishonesty to be rampant,
with 75 percent of surveyed undergraduates admitting to cheating (Bowers,
1964). Around that same time, colleges and universities began to institute
conduct policies to convey "that absolute integrity is expected of every student
and that it is wrong to fraudulently or unfairly advance with academic status
or knowingly be a party to another student failure to maintain academic
integrity" (Columbia Weighs an Honor System, 1963, par. 3).

Despite widely implemented "regulatory responses" (LaFollette, 1999) in
postsecondary education institutions, a multi-institutional study conducted
in the 1990s reported that academic dishonesty among undergraduates continued to be problematic at rates equal to, if not higher than, those found in
the 1960s (McCabe, 1992, 1993; McCabe and Trevino, 1993). The research
findings of McCabe and others stimulated a varied group of faculty and
student affairs administrators (including Donald McCabe of Rutgers University, Gary Pavela of the University of Maryland, and Bill Kibler, then of Texas
A&M University) to form the Center for Academic Integrity (CAI) in 1992.
The aim of the CAI, now affiliated with the Rutland Institute of Ethics
at Clemson University, is to "identify, affirm, and promote the values of
academic integrity among students, faculty, teachers, and administrators"
(www.academicintegrity.org). Since 1992, a steady supply of scholarly, popular,
and associated press publications have evoked academic integrity as a solution

to student academic misconduct (Dannells, 1997; Kibler, Nuss, Paterson, and Pavela, 1988; Whitley and Keith-Spiegel, 2002; Wilson, 1999).

Academic integrity has routinely been called on in times of perceived crises in postsecondary education. In 1929 a dean of Rutgers University beseeched matriculated students to uphold academic integrity because it "prohibits all bigotry either of science, philosophy or religion . . . under the conviction that in truth and truth alone is found the freedom and progress of the human race" ("Fifty-Eight Get Rutgers Degrees," 1929, p. 23). In 1979 corporate executives and politicians called for academic integrity to be restored in response to "plagiarism by students and teachers; conflicts of interests among researchers and scholars; [and] imposition of unjustified course requirements merely to improve the colleges cash balances" (Hechinger, 1979, p. C1). One year later, the Pac-10 Conference claimed protection of academic integrity when it declared five member schools ineligible to compete as a consequence of fraudulent behaviors such as "unearned credits, falsified transcripts and unwarranted intrusion of athletic department interest into the academic processes ("Five in Pac-10 Rules Ineligible in Football," 1980, p. D17).

Claims of a decline in academic integrity continue to be made regularly in the twenty-first century (Boynton, 2001; Eckstein, 2003; Haynes and Berkowitz, 2007). The intent of these academic integrity evocations by administrative and public authorities is to quell the moral panic and state expectations for legitimate academic conduct. The purpose of academic integrity is to highlight the expectation that truth, academic freedom, courage, quality, and the spirit of free intellectual inquiry will guide the academic work of students and faculty ("College Ousts Student for Plagiarism," 1965; Evans and Novak, 1970).

Fears of a Cheating Culture

A moral panic exists in the twenty-first century about the existence of a "cheating culture" (Callahan, 2004) in high schools, colleges, and universities. Recent reports suggest that student cheating, research fraud, faculty plagiarism, and administrator fraud in schools and universities around the world is normative and slowly corrupting the integrity of the educative enterprise (Anglen, 2006;

Callahan, 2004; Decoo, 2002; Eckstein, 2003; Hallak and Poisson, 2007; Monastersky, 2006; Ray, 2006; Sims, 1993). The most extensive research has been conducted on academic misconduct among students, while less is known about misconduct among researchers, faculty, and administrators (in that order). A more thorough note of caution in interpreting misconduct research is presented later, but for now it is important to understand that misconduct statistics are most often derived from self-reported and perceptional data and so less is known about actual rates of misconduct.

Survey studies on student academic misconduct suggest that as few as 1 percent and as many as 90 percent of students self-report engagement in behaviors such as using other people's words and ideas without attribution, working with others on independently assigned work, and copying from other students during examinations (Brimble and Stevenson-Clarke, 2006; Christensen Hughes and McCabe, 2006; McCabe and Trevino, 1997). The lower rates of engagement are usually associated with "more serious" forms of cheating such as hiring an examination proxy or writing an assignment for another student (Brimble and Stevenson-Clarke, 2006).

Less is known about misconduct among faculty, researchers, and administrators because few empirical studies have been conducted and "the general practice is to treat reports and results of investigations with great confidentiality" (Eckstein, 2003, p. 42). It is suspected that, similar to that among students, more serious forms of misconduct (for example, fraud) are not extraordinarily high among faculty and researchers but that the bending of norms, "misbehaving," or "sloppy science" may be quite common (Braxton and Mann, 2004; DeVries, Anderson, and Martinson, 2006; Steneck, 1992, cited in Louis, Anderson, and Rosenberg, 1995). Braxton and Mann (2004) found that of 4,200 students surveyed, however, under 20 percent observed norm violations (such as inattentive planning, particularistic grading) by their instructors. And Louis, Anderson, and Rosenberg (1995) found that researchers report observing misconduct over a five-year period by, on average, only three people. But according to the Office of Research Integrity, "the number of institutions responding to allegations of research misconduct has grown steadily from 1992–2001 and is expected to continue to do so" (Rhoades, 2004, p. 11).

Even less is known about misconduct among administrators, although an increased number of reports in the popular press and revelations of administrative scandals imply there is a reason to be concerned (Eckstein, 2003; Field, 2007; Hallak and Poisson, 2007; Su and Magee, 2007). Some of the more publicized accounts of late are those at Southern Illinois (Lederman, 2006), University of Texas at Austin (Field, 2007), and Maricopa Community College (Anglen, 2006), with incidents ranging from plagiarism of institutional strategic plans to conflicts of interest and more serious fraudulent acts such as falsified enrollment numbers and theft of college money and equipment. Corruption at the highest levels of the institution is all the more devastating because the public depends on organizational leadership to self-regulate and model integrity for the institution as a whole (El-Khawas, 1979).

Despite the lack of empirical evidence demonstrating that an unacceptable level of corruption has been reached, interest in prevention (through ethics education and policy implementation), policing, and severe punishment of misconduct has been growing steadily. It is argued that corrupt practices among students, teachers, researchers, and administrators have a tremendous impact on the integrity of the educational enterprise and thus even a low level of corruption cannot be tolerated (Hallak and Poisson, 2007). In response, many universities, including the University of California and Southern Illinois University, have implemented ethics tutorials for their employees. Other universities are revising their academic and research integrity policies in the aftermath of publicized scandals (Lederman, 2005). Educational measures, policies, and procedures being implemented on postsecondary education campuses are intended to manage individual conduct by emphasizing personal integrity and encouraging conduct that complies with institutional rules.

Time for a New Approach

Despite these laudable organizational efforts, a real (or perceived) problem of academic misconduct in colleges and universities continues (Eckstein, 2003; Hallak and Poisson, 2007; McCabe, 2005a). If corruption is indeed as systemic and pervasive as to warrant fears of a cheating culture, the usefulness of current organizational approaches is questionable (Bertram Gallant, 2006;

Conrad, 2006; Howard, 2001; Maruca, 2003; Puka, 2005; Townley and Parsell, 2004). Organizational approaches to academic misconduct should take into account the organizational tensions and societal forces that complicate the work of students and faculty (Barnett and Dalton, 1981; Hall and Kuh, 1998; Howard, 2001; Whicker and Kronenfeld, 1994). And although some have highlighted the complexity of postsecondary education in the twenty-first century (Bok, 2003; Kezar, Chambers, and Burkhardt, 2005), the way in which it shapes academic integrity has not yet been fully explored.

This monograph is timely because interests in academic integrity as well as the teaching and learning imperative are emerging to the forefront of international dialogues and potentially converging. As student affairs professionals and faculty seek ways to enhance academic integrity on campus, other associations and campus centers are seeking ways to stimulate learning-oriented environments, highlight the learning imperative of postsecondary education, and improve assessments and accreditation processes (Association of American Colleges and Universities, 2004; Astin, 1996; Keeling, 2004; Schroeder, 1996). This convergence may have been in the making for some time. The historical examination of academic integrity in this monograph demonstrates that student academic conduct has always been strongly connected to faculty work, institutional structures, context, and organizational pressures. Student affairs professionals, faculty, and other campus constituents who have struggled with reducing academic misconduct and enhancing academic integrity may find their practices reinvigorated by the new organizational strategy posited in this monograph that links academic integrity to the teaching and learning imperative of the twenty-first century postsecondary educational system.

The Context for a New Approach

Current organizational approaches to student academic misconduct can be characterized in the form of a question: How do we stop students from cheating? In the quest to stop students from cheating, organizations trend toward two dominant strategies—rule compliance and integrity (Paine, 1994; Whitley and Keith-Spiegel, 2002). In the rule compliance strategy, the focus is on the articulation of rules for responsible conduct and enforcement of those rules, primarily through disciplining misconduct. The aim of the integrity strategy is to develop in students the character necessary to resist misconduct and the fortitude to choose actions that align with institutional rules even at a detriment to self-interests. Both of these strategies are well embedded in the student affairs profession, which emerged to manage and control college student conduct but has now evolved to include developing the whole student and partnering with faculty in the improvement of the learning environment (Rentz, 1996; Schroeder, 1996).

Yet the dominant organizational strategies generate tensions that undermine the learning imperative and create chasms between students and faculty as well as between faculty and student affairs. The strains—on the faculty-student relationship, the role of faculty, the learning process, ideas of teaching and learning, and student development—inhibit the effectiveness of the dominant strategies. The existence of these strains, combined with the resiliency of student academic misconduct despite organizational efforts, demands a new approach that tackles the multidimensional nature of the issue. This new approach reframes the driving question from "how do we stop students from cheating?" to "how do we ensure students are learning?"

Asking "how do we ensure students are learning?" is congruent with the current context of postsecondary education. First is the increasing attention of the student affairs profession on the learning mission of the postsecondary education institution (Astin, 1996). Student affairs professionals make up the campus group most consistently concerned with students' conduct. They have also been the group that advocated for the move from discipline to development in addressing students' misconduct (Dannells, 1997). At the beginning of the twenty-first century, the student affairs profession has once again called attention to the potential of the university campus to affect the whole student, this time through the creation of transformative learning experiences (Keeling, 2004). Attending to academic integrity through a teaching and learning strategy, then, is aligned with the broader student affairs vision of reconsidering learning in postsecondary education.

Second are the increasing public and political pressures for greater accountability of colleges and universities to stay true to their teaching and learning missions (Association of American Colleges and Universities, 2004). The general public, concerned about the rising cost and importance of a postsecondary education, is increasingly demanding greater transparency regarding college learning outcomes and connections between class work and student learning (Hallak and Poisson, 2007). Such public demands are translating into new governmental interference in the operations of postsecondary education institutions (for example, the Spellings Commission in the United States). The time of unqualified trust in educators and the educational system may be gone: "Attitudes toward educators nowadays are often ambivalent and contradictory: admiring and respectful toward those held to be bearers of truth and knowledge, and at the same time negative and cynical about their roles and behaviour" (Eckstein, 2003, p. 19).

This lens through which postsecondary education institutions are being viewed magnifies the importance of attending to student academic integrity in the larger framework of teaching and learning. This larger framework reflects that academic integrity is a broader issue than can be relegated to student affairs; it specifically calls for faculty to be more intentionally and intimately involved in the generation of solutions. In addition, concerns with institutional corruption at all levels (student, faculty, and administration) are coalescing into an acknowledgment that people's actions—ethical and unethical—are in part shaped by the actions of others as well as by institutional and cultural contexts (Hallak and Poisson, 2007).

Organizational strategies that incorporate methods for stopping cheating but are sufficiently expansive to enhance the possibilities for fulfillment of the postsecondary education mission must be devised. Asking how we ensure that students are learning begs additional questions not necessarily considered in the focus on stopping students from cheating such as "how do we ensure faculty are teaching?" and "how do ensure institutional structures and cultures support integrity in teaching and learning?" These additional questions acknowledge the interaction of individual agencies, institutional structures, and organizational cultures and thus propel more robust organizational strategies and calls for a view of academic integrity that goes beyond students' cheating.

Interpreting Misconduct Research

Literature published in the last decade conveys the impression that academic misconduct has become problematic beyond an acceptable level of corruption:

"Nowadays, the number and range of dubious practices have extended to widespread misconduct, individual and systematic, organizational and institutional" (Eckstein, 2003, p. 18). Callahan (2004) also suggests in the *Cheating Culture* that "more Americans are doing wrong to get ahead," and surveys by McCabe and others tend to suggest that as many as 95 percent of students today engage in misconduct (McCabe and Trevino, 1996). The numbers and statistics, however, should be interpreted with caution for three reasons.

First, the majority of studies from which the figures are derived are surveys of self-reported behaviors. It is difficult to know, therefore, the actual extent to which people do engage in misconduct; "it is well-known that respondents are not always truthful when presented with surveys that ask them questions regarding sensitive, illegal, or socially unacceptable behaviors" (Cizek, 2003, p. 5). Experimental studies on student academic misconduct have demonstrated much lower rates than survey studies—as low as 3 percent (Eisenberg, 2004; Karlins, Michaels, and Podlogar, 1988; Weber, McBee, and Krebs, 1983). Experimental studies, however, are generally limited to in-class test situations, while survey studies tend to ask about all types of academic behaviors, including those that occur outside the classroom such as plagiarism and "unauthorized collaboration" on homework assignments. As a result, self-report rates are naturally higher than those found in experimental studies.

This observation leads to the second area for caution: survey studies that report the percentage of people who "cheat" misrepresent the empirical evidence. Survey results can only suggest that respondents may be engaging in behaviors that may be considered cheating by their educational institutions. Little evidence exists that people share common definitions of cheating (Brimble and Stevenson-Clarke, 2006; Seriup Pincus and Pedhazur Schmelkin, 2003). Thus, research validity is further lessened by those survey studies that only ask respondents whether they "cheat" rather than whether they engage in specific behaviors (for example, use cheat sheets in examinations, copy and paste without attribution). And when responses are parceled out, far fewer students report engaging in those behaviors they consider "serious misconduct" than in those behaviors they consider "less serious" (Baird, 1980; Barnett and Dalton, 1981; McCabe and Pavela, 2000). In other words, some of the contemporary concerns with the state of academic integrity are based on the way in which readers interpret the word "cheat" and the images invoked by what may be a value-laden term.

This issue leads to the third area for caution. The language used to convey the results of these survey study results can powerfully influence public reactions and institutional responses. Most of the survey studies on academic misconduct report the findings more conclusively than the actually are, alluding to the existence of a "cheating culture." For example, McCabe and Pavela (2000) report that 68 percent of students at campuses without honor codes engage in serious cheating, but a more accurate statement would be "68 percent of surveyed students admit to engaging in a behavior considered serious cheating at least once during their college career." The second statement seems less urgent and dire than the earlier one, given that many people could likely admit to having engaged in a questionable behavior at least once in their lives. Whether misconduct in the academy is any more of a problem now than it has ever been is rather unknown because of these three validity issues (Burrus, McGoldrick, and Schuhmann, 2007).

A Note on Definitions

The terms used in the discussion of academic integrity and academic misconduct vary according to publishing outlet and audience. Consistent across discourses, however, is the representation of the issue in ethical binaries: honesty-dishonesty, wrong-right, immoral-moral, unethical-ethical, and bad-good (Valentine, 2006). Common terms synonymous with misconduct include "academic dishonesty," "cheating," "fraud," "falsification," and "plagiarism," while "honor" and "honesty" are terms used interchangeably with academic integrity.

The student academic conduct literature of late has been most persistent in perpetuating this moral dichotomy. In fact, the use of the terms "academic integrity" and "academic dishonesty" seems contained in the literature on student academic conduct and seldom used in the literature on the conduct of other organizational members. For instance, in inquiries of research conduct, the more common terms are "research misconduct" and "responsible research conduct." In the broader arena of administration and teaching, the language at the integrity end of the continuum includes "ethical conduct," "compliance," and "accountability," while at the other end the terms used are "improprieties," "administrator misconduct," "professorial misconduct," and "teaching misconduct."

This monograph uses the term "academic integrity" synonymously with "institutional integrity," denoting coherency between promises or rhetoric and actions. "Academic misconduct" is used to refer to behaviors that undermine academic integrity because they do not comply with rules, norms, or expectations. At times, when deemed appropriate to reflect the cited author's meaning, morally laden words such as "cheating," "honesty," and "dishonesty" are also used.

Delineating Forms of Academic Misconduct

The behaviors thought to undermine academic integrity are numerous and defined differently across different contexts and audiences. At the local level, instructors can define student academic misconduct in particular classrooms, and deans can define faculty misconduct in particular departments. At the global level, organizations and associations can define faculty, researcher, and administrator misconduct. Most notably, the National Institutes of Health (NIH) and the National Science Foundation (NSF) are able to define misconduct in research projects funded through their organizations. Because the authority to define misconduct is vested in multiple parties, the definitions are diverse. A review of available literature and documents, however, suggests that the following academic misconduct terms transcend group boundaries and roles:

- Plagiarism—using another's words or ideas without appropriate attribution or without following citation conventions;
- Fabrication—making up data, results, information, or numbers, and recording and reporting them;
- Falsification—manipulating research, data, or results to inaccurately portray information in reports (research, financial, or other) or academic assignments;

- Misrepresentation—falsely representing oneself, efforts, or abilities; and,
- Misbehavior—acting in ways that are not overtly misconduct but are counter to prevailing behavioral expectations.

Examples of behaviors that fall under each category differ based on the roles being performed. In the role of student, people are expected to learn and demonstrate their independent abilities and knowledge. Thus, misrepresentation by students includes unauthorized collaboration and use of unauthorized aids in completing academic assignments, whereas falsification by students can include altering a graded examination in an attempt to earn additional points. In the role of teacher, people are expected to teach and fairly evaluate student learning. Thus, misrepresentation by teachers can include inattentive planning and a cynical attitude toward teaching, while misbehavior by teachers may include unarticulated or ambiguous expectations and personal disregard (for example, consistently being late to class).

An implicit distinction exists between those behaviors that bend social norms (misbehavior) and those that transcend ethical boundaries toward fraud and even crime (misconduct), but it is not normally delineated in student conduct policies (Howard, 2000a). Clearly, researchers who falsify research, students who pay others as examination proxies, and administrators who falsify financial records are corrupting the educational institution with fraudulent behaviors. Other "misbehaviors" are a concern not because they break laws or clearly defy institutional expectations but because they slowly erode the teaching, learning, and research environment (Louis, Anderson, and Rosenberg, 1995).

Summary

An academic integrity movement is afoot in postsecondary education institutions in the United States, Canada, and beyond. This movement has tended to focus on the conduct and character of students and thus positioned students and student affairs professionals as the key actors. This monograph suggests, however, that it is time for a new approach that broadens the movement beyond student conduct and character to the teaching and learning environment. In proposing this broad-based approach, this monograph does not suggest that misconduct be treated lightly or remain undisciplined but that integrity is multidimensional, shaped by many more forces than the actions of the student body, and that colleges and universities should attend to integrity at all these levels.

This monograph is intended for student affairs professionals, students, faculty, academic administrators, presidents, and governing officers who are poised to renew their commitment to enhancing academic integrity on their campuses and challenge traditional organizational strategies. It is for the student affairs professional who looks to build partnerships with faculty, libraries, and teaching centers on campus to broaden campus dialogue beyond student conduct. It is for faculty who wish to highlight to administration the institutional constraints inhibiting their ability to enhance the integrity of their teaching environments. The material in this monograph can be used to stimulate campus dialogue and initiate a robust approach to academic integrity.

In positing a teaching and learning strategy, I readily acknowledge the difficulties organizations will face in making the transition from strategies rooted in the history of postsecondary education and embedded in the divided roles of faculty and student affairs. I respond to that concern by providing ideas for implementation, though each campus will experience its own struggles. Before turning to these strategies, I explore the lengthy history of student academic misconduct and the way in which postsecondary education organizations have traditionally responded to it.

Revisiting the Past: The Historical Context of Academic Integrity

> *In the matter of classroom honesty, we make the conservative estimate that at least half the Yale undergraduates are at this moment guilty of breaking the college rules during the present exam period, the penalty for which is expulsion, the description . . . cheating.*
>
> ["Cheating at Yale," 1930, par. 1]

IN THE SUBTITLE of *The Cheating Culture*, Callahan (2004) suggests that "more Americans are doing wrong to get ahead." This argument is partly based on survey results demonstrating that a majority of high school and post-secondary students report engaging in academic misconduct (McCabe and Trevino, 1996). Yet as the previous quote illustrates, student cheating is certainly not a new phenomenon in postsecondary education. If student cheating is not a new phenomenon, several questions are intimated. Why is it perceived that students are cheating at this time more than at any other time in history? Have there been other times when a "moral panic" about student cheating has surfaced, and, if so, what events led to it?

This chapter explores these questions by examining scholarly and popular press reports and portrayals of academic integrity, cheating, and corruption in the history of American postsecondary education. Popular press pieces were included as a window into public perceptions of academic integrity, and scholarly pieces, in complement, illuminate the ways in which the academy has viewed academic integrity over time. For each period of history (adapted from Lucas, 1994; Thelin, 2004; Ward, 2003), I review the institutional context pertaining to conduct and discipline, predominant definitions of misconduct, and organizational approaches to misconduct.

The Antebellum Period: 1760–1860

Antebellum colleges and universities were characterized by routine classroom structures (lectures were followed by recitations and students were assessed daily on their memorization of course material) and stringent rules and policies (Allmendinger, 1973; Chipman and McDonald, 1982; Lucas, 1994; Moore, 1978; Thelin, 2004; Wagoner, 1986). The routine pedagogy as well as the adversarial relationships between faculty and students is thought to have encouraged students to use methods such as cribbing or cheat sheets to survive (Allmendinger, 1973; Lucas, 1994). The adversarial relationships were created because the stringent rules and policies had to be monitored and enforced by tutors and professors (Chipman and McDonald, 1982; Lucas, 1994; Moore, 1978; Thelin, 2004). This crime-and-punishment system of discipline was a leftover from earlier residential colleges in which students lived with and among their professors (Allmendinger, 1973).

It was during the antebellum period that colleges and universities implemented the use of grades to rank students, and the modern system of discipline was created (Allmendinger, 1973; Hessinger, 1999). It was expected that grading and ranking the students would "demand self-control, and would exact a routine of its own to replace the institutional procedures of the lost collegiate community" (Allmendinger, 1973, p. 82). The penalties applied for misconduct in the antebellum period included removal from campus and lowering of rank. The penalties were considered effective deterrents for misconduct, as the market demand for university graduates was high. The effectiveness of these deterrents, however, was likely mitigated by the ease with which removed students could purchase degrees from one of the many diploma mills that emerged during this time in history (Thelin, 2004).

Misconduct Defined

Antebellum misconduct seems best defined as disorder—defying campus authorities, including classroom teachers, by lying, cheating, or stealing

(Allmendinger, 1973). For example, at the College of William and Mary in Virginia, which is the first institution thought to develop an honor code, misconduct was described as telling a lie or doing anything else "contrary to good manners" (William and Mary Student Handbook, 2007–2008). In this sense, misconduct was delineated by its breadth rather than its specificity during the antebellum era.

Organizational Approaches

Antebellum colleges approached misconduct in a way similar to contemporary approaches—through the implementation and enforcement of conduct codes. There were codes of conduct for every facet of the student life, from dress to classroom decorum, which reflected perhaps the earliest version of in loco parentis (Allmendinger, 1973). Deans of men and women positions were created to manage these codes and student conduct in general (Rentz, 1996).

Wagoner (1986) and Pace (2004) reveal, however, that the original college honor code was not enacted first by faculty or deans of students but originated from the students and the southern culture of the time. This southern honor code was "a set of rules that advanced the appearance of duty, pride, power, and self-esteem; and conformity to these rules [was] required if an individual [was] to be considered and honorable member of society" (Pace, 2004, p. 4). In other words, the preservation of honor originally meant preserving self-worth and personal reputation, not protecting or obeying institutional rules (Pace, 2004; Thelin, 2004; Wagoner, 1986). For example, at the University of Virginia, a contemporary honor code school, the original code defined "academic citizenship" as "never betraying a fellow student" (Thelin, 2004, p. 52). The South Carolina College honor code also protected against "insults to personal honor" and was considered "a rehearsal for adult public life" (Thelin, 2004, p. 49).

The honor code in the antebellum era, then, could actually be cited by a student to justify his cheating, especially if his honor was being threatened by failure in a course or public humiliation by his teacher. In other words, "when faced with the possibility of humiliation, the Southern code recognized that saving face is more important than conforming to moral or ethical standards of behavior" (Pace, 2004, p. 27). Historically, then, cheating was considered an honorable way for students "to cope with the potential humiliation represented by the faculty, the curriculum, and the teaching methods" (Pace, 2004, p. 28) and the "'clashes of honor' between the faculty and the students" (Wagoner, 1986, p. 165). Antebellum colleges and universities originally responded to such student conduct using grading and ranking systems to discipline student misconduct (Hessinger, 1999). The student honor code was eventually co-opted, however, by research era colleges and universities.

The Research University: 1860–1945

The era of the research university is the era of utilitarian education—education for the people and the government—marked partially by the Morrill Act (Hessinger, 1999; Thelin, 2004; Ward, 2003). During this era, the student population grew in size and diversified as women began attending normal colleges in preparation for teaching careers. Although the Morrill Act of 1862 was intended to extend postsecondary education to all, funding was insufficient and so there was very little institutional change until the beginning of the twentieth century (Thelin, 2004). It was at the beginning of the twentieth century that the research university began to be realized and the contemporary teaching, research, and service mission born.

The production of knowledge through original research became increasingly emphasized as an American educative imperative during this period. Thus, the "emphasis of faculty work shifted from teaching to teaching and research, with research beginning to be seen as the prime contributor to a faculty member's professional status" (Ward, 2003, p. 33). The passing of the Copyright Act in 1909 represents the increasing interest in knowledge production and "greater administrative oversight of student writing activities in a general effort both to curb potential copyright infringement and to teach the spirit of the new law" (Marsh, 2004, p. 80).

Emphasis on the production of knowledge and the division of faculty into academic disciplines and areas of expertise fed into an emerging hierarchical system of institutional ranking; the "great American universities" such as Harvard, Johns Hopkins, and Cornell were compared with the standard universities, which lacked wealth and expertise (Thelin, 2004). Also emerging during this period was the "California idea" of postsecondary education that positioned colleges and universities to "educate future generations of enlightened, capable state leaders and citizens" to counter widespread political and corporate corruption (Thelin, 2004, p. 139).

Although a concern with student conduct was not a new phenomenon in this era, "new perceptions of moral decay, institutional failure, and general cultural anomie prompted a marked increase in urgency" (Setran, 2005, p. 207). Despite the promise of morally evolved graduates, campus life was marked by a "juvenile" student population that studied little and worked even less (Lucas, 1994). By the 1930s, students were heavily involved in extracurricular and political activities, and student affairs professionals became fully integrated on campus as the managers of student life (Lucas, 1994; Thelin, 2004). As a result, students were perceived to be lacking in intellectual curiosity or interest in their academic work because they spent the majority of their time outside the classroom in leisure activities rather than in study (Angell, 1928).

The growing interest in production of original knowledge among college and university faculty correlated with an increasing expectation that students also would be interested and engaged in it. This expectation was largely unmet, precipitating an intellectual divide between students and their teachers. Angell (1928) credits this divide and students' lack of intellectual interest to the research orientation of the faculty (whose teaching is thus "dry, pedantic, [and] boring") and to institutional forms such as corporate bureaucracies, academic divisions, definite subject curricula, large lecture classes, and examination testing. These institutional structures and pedagogical changes not only de-emphasized learning but created new opportunities for cheating. Students could easily obtain an advance copy of the examination from a friend and write the examination answers in the examination booklet (which students had to supply) before the scheduled examination time (Marsh, 2004).

The classroom thus became the site of a game of war between students and faculty to see who could outwit the other:

> *Many young men and women who are scrupulously honorable in other relationships of life seem to have little hesitancy in submitting themes and theses which they have not written, in bringing prepared "cribs" to examinations, and in conveying information to one*

another during the course of an examination. There is a not uncommon feeling that a state of war exists between faculty members and students . . . partly explained by the unsympathetic attitude of some professors, and partly by the rather mechanical organization involving grades, warnings, and probation; but, certainly, the principal cause must be found in the failure of undergraduates to appreciate the value to themselves of serious and conscientious intellectual effort and achievement [Angell, 1928, p. 44].

Despite anecdotal and research reports that a significant percentage of students (around 40 percent) admitted to academic "cheating," expressed public concern over the conduct of students was rare during this period (Drake, 1941; Jacob, 1957; Parr, 1936).

Misconduct Defined

Student cheating or "cribbing" (using cheat sheets) on oral, recitation, and standard examinations was commonly discussed and considered quite commonplace during the research university era. It was well known that students used cheat sheets and stole exam questions ahead of time (Angell, 1928; Pace, 2004). In general, though, it seems that student cheating was perceived less as a criminal or immoral act and more as "charming foolery" (Briggs, 1969, p. 31) or the "folly" of the inexperienced and incompetent "college boy" ("The Folly of Plagiarism," 1901). Concern over student academic misconduct may have been minimal during this time because predominant institutional structures such as small class sizes and oral examinations presented limited opportunities for cheating or plagiarism. The characterization of student cheating as "follies" may also have been in part related to the belief that little harm came to others when a student copied or cribbed in an examination or paper. This relaxed attitude toward student academic misconduct quickly dissipated as large classes and written assessments became more commonplace.

Organizational Approaches

It was at the beginning of this postsecondary education era when the southern honor code was translated into an early version of the contemporary "honor system," replacing honor among peers with honor to the institution (Bowman, 2006). Postsecondary education institutions co-opted the traditional honor code in an attempt to harness the peer power in the direction of institutional rule compliance rather than defiance. Haverford College's honor system, for example, was initiated in 1896 to identify "the behaviors considered to be intellectually dishonorable, such as cheating on examinations, copying another person's papers, talking about an examination that other students have not yet taken," and put the responsibility of monitoring cheating in the hands of the students (Heath, 1968, p. 37). Similar to Haverford College, Princeton adopted the honor system in 1892–93 in the belief that it was the best way to deal with student cheating. In a 1905 *New York Times* article, Woodrow Wilson, then president of Princeton, was cited as describing the honor system as "the practice of conducting examinations . . . under the self-direction of the pupils themselves, depending for the prevention of cheating . . . upon the honorable as esprit de corps of the young men or boys who are undergoing the ordeal" (par. 1).

The shift in responsibility for academic integrity from faculty to students is not surprising, given the shift in responsibilities of faculty from teaching to teaching and research. Faculty and administrators also felt that with the increased use of written assessments that were completed outside the classroom, it would be difficult for anyone other than the students to enforce academic honesty (Briggs, 1969). The necessity of student enforcement was promulgated even in the popular press. A 1931 article publicly reprimands Yale for repealing the honor code in favor of relying on authoritative enforcement of rules because, the editorial argues, if the pressure for honor does not come from "the students as a community," the notion of honor will be lost. The belief in the power of the honor system to control student behavior was strong: "the honor system is a potentially powerful psychological determinant and regulator of behavior. . . . There is little doubt that most students strongly support the academic code and perceive any willful concerted attempt to subvert its spirit to be a threat to their own freedom and moral integrity" (Heath, 1968, p. 38).

Despite such honor code proponents, student misconduct continued to be problematic throughout the research university era. Angell argued that honor systems were ineffective in universities with large lecture classes because the "ethical morale" of the students was low and honor unlikely to be enforced (Angell, 1928, p. 220). Popular and scholarly publications began calling for college administrators to step in and enforce the conduct codes; "the fact that so-called honor systems are failing to function effectively in so many of our institutions should cause college administrators to give serious consideration to this problem" (Parr, 1936, p. 318). So toward the end of this era, student code enforcement in class was gradually augmented by techniques such as spacing students apart in examinations, and disallowing notes and books at the student's desk: "to prevent hired professionals from being substituted for undergraduates, students taking examinations at Long Island University last week were required to present identification cards with their photographs attached" ("Cheating at Long Island," 1930, par. 1). Student monitoring, however, was still largely depended on for enforcing the conduct code during completion of homework assignments and other out-of-class academic work because neither faculty nor administrators would be present to monitor and report student cheating.

Mass Education: 1945–1975

This thirty-year period of postsecondary education was marked most profoundly by the massive "expansion and diversification of the student body (and the faculty) as new opportunities arose for students of diverse socioeconomic classes, races, ages, abilities and gender" (Ward, 2003, p. 36). This expansion and resulting diversification pushed postsecondary education into the public and political spotlight and emphasized the new philosophy that education was a right rather than a privilege (Thelin, 2004; Ward, 2003). This right to education was loosely realized, however, as the hierarchy in prestige developed in the previous era became more pronounced in this era. There was a growing gap between the "elite" colleges and universities that served a select portion of the population (usually white and middle to upper class) and the community colleges that enrolled the remaining students.

Yet the GI bill and increased funding for postsecondary education created a postsecondary education system that had to become more responsive to students' and the public's needs. As a result, the public's, the government's, and the students' questioning of the accountability of postsecondary education institutions and their faculty intensified. Students became more vocal in administrative affairs, and campus turmoil was commonplace in the sixties and early seventies. According to Thelin (2004), the fights and extreme positions of the student body versus the administrative body "shrank the middle ground for the genuine, appropriate teaching and learning that were part of the university ideal, if not always the reality" (p. 310).

Some writers suggest that academic misconduct was a direct outcome of the rapid expansion of postsecondary education "during the turbulent decade from 1964–1974 that included Watergate and Vietnam" ("What Price Honor?" 1976). Most notably, litigations and scandals involving academic scientists led to concerns over research integrity that inform contemporary research ethics codes, rules for human subjects research, and research integrity programs and offices throughout the academy. In addition, several heavily publicized student cheating scandals from 1964 to 1975 at the Air Force Academy, University of Florida, and University of Wisconsin leveraged public questioning of the effectiveness of honor codes and the ability of postsecondary education institutions to control the student body ("Cheating in Florida," 1975; Hechinger, 1965; McGrath, 1982; Pollard, 1972; Roark, 1981).

A 1971 exposé by *The Boston Globe* on the rising term paper industry and the subsequent allegations against 600 students at the University of Wisconsin were perhaps the events that finally pushed the public and campuses to consider student academic misconduct as normative and indicative of a cheating crisis (Pollard, 1972; Trachtenberg, 1972). The term paper industry was of significant concern because it exponentially increased access to cheating resources, particularly for paper assignments (Amsden, 1977; Lamont, 1979; Pollard, 1972; Sewall and Drake, 1980; Trachtenberg, 1972). The "recycling" of old essay themes and examination questions by faculty was well known on college campuses; so too was the availability of previously written (and graded) papers and examinations, predominantly in fraternity or sorority files (Haviland and Mullin, 1999; Simmons, 1999). Emergence of the term paper industry, however, offered increased access for students who lacked the on-campus cultural capital that came with group membership. The public seemed to recognize the ramifications of this enhanced access; during this time in history, there was at least a doubling of publications on academic misconduct and publicized skepticism on the integrity of the academic enterprise (Connell, 1981; Sewall and Drake, 1980; Trachtenberg, 1972).

Making the Grade (Becker, Geer, and Hughes, 1968) is perhaps one of the seminal pieces on student conduct published during this era. The authors connect institutional context with student behavior and conclude their sociological study with the following point: student misconduct is in reaction to a lack of control or say into institutional structures and systems. In response to this lack of power, students form a collective and act in a collective sense; they "arrive at common definitions of their situation and give shared meanings to the people and contingencies they confront" and work together to "deal with their problems of academic work" (p. 132). Students "cheat," then, to rectify perceived wrongs against them, specifically illegitimate institutional constraints on their ability to earn high grades. Shaffer (1966) also noted that institutional features such as the pressure for good grades and the blurry lines of academic misconduct contributed to cheating behaviors during the mass education era: specifically, "too much pressure . . . on good students to get top grades and pressure on poor students to avoid flunking out. Parents are often blamed for pushing offspring beyond their capacities; students have said they would rather cheat than disappoint families with mediocre or failing grades" (Shaffer, 1966, p. 349).

It may be important to call attention to the parallel trend between the demographic changes in the student population and the intensifying interests in expanding the definitions of academic misconduct and stopping students from cheating. Much of the literature would suggest that this parallel existed because more students were cheating more, but other writers argue that "cultural differences between students and their professors, whether ethnic, cultural, geographical or generational" may be at play (Maruca, 2005, p. 244). (The influence of diversity on the complexity of academic integrity is considered later in the monograph.)

Misconduct Defined

Around the beginning of the mass education era, academic misconduct was still defined as cheating but had expanded to include copying papers along with cheating on and cribbing examinations. The term "academic dishonesty" began to appear more regularly in the popular and scholarly press during this period. One of the first popular appearances of *academic integrity* in reference to student integrity also occurred during this time. A *New York Times* article in 1963 reported on the Commission on Academic Integrity at Columbia College. The commission, according to the article, was established to institute an academic integrity pledge to convey "that absolute integrity is expected of every student, and that it is wrong to fraudulently or unfairly advance with academic status or knowingly be a party to another student's failure to maintain academic integrity" ("Columbia Weighs an Honor System, 1963, par. 3). Since the mass education era, academic integrity has increasingly come to represent student integrity in educational rhetoric.

This narrowing of academic integrity from institutional to student integrity may have played a role in two trends on postsecondary education campuses. The first trend is the separation of students' integrity from that of faculty, researchers, or administrators, with separate policies and codes guiding each body. The second trend is the relative neglect of organizational, institutional, and societal dimensions of the issue compared with the student character and integrity dimension. Each trend is examined in more detail later in the monograph. For now, it is important to note that the contemporary use of academic integrity as student integrity has a relatively short history in American postsecondary education.

Organizational Approaches

Widespread institutional movement to discipline students' cheating on class examinations occurred in the 1960s. Numerous popular press reports conveyed public interest in student academic misconduct. A *New York Times* piece in 1960 reported that the University of Alabama administration punished eighty-six students for cheating, including "illegal entries into the professor's offices for the purposes of securing examinations and . . . buying and selling tests" ("Eighty-Six Cheaters Punished," 1960, par. 4). In that same year, the University of California, Los Angeles, responded to massive cribbing and plagiarism by creating a "statement of principle on cheating, plagiarism, and classroom dishonesty" to convey that "the University cannot condone cheating" (Dash, 1960, p. WS1). This media trend condemning the increase in student cheating and reporting on the responses of colleges and universities continued through the next era (Akst, 1987; Fishbein, 1993; Hechinger, 1965; Morrison, 1976; Pollard, 1972; Rafferty, 1965; Roark, 1981; Tolchin, 1965).

It is not surprising that around this same time colleges and universities began to legislate en masse policies and procedures regarding academic integrity. This movement was likely in response to a perception of widespread cheating, the students' lack of willingness to self-monitor, and judicial demands that students accused of academic misconduct be afforded due process ("Cheating in Colleges," 1976; "Cheating in Exams," 1967; Lamont, 1979). To avoid turning academic discipline over to the courts, colleges and universities began to uniformly institute university-administered discipline and due process procedures to back up student-run honor codes. And by the 1970s traditional honor codes appeared to have generally lost favor in all but the historic institutions: "changing attitudes and academic pressures had made the codes all but outmoded on many campuses" (Students Find College Honor Codes Losing Favor, 1975, par. 2).

The varied types, sizes, and missions of higher education institutions may have negated the effectiveness of a uniform approach to addressing student academic misconduct. Honor codes persisted in the military academies, in smaller religious schools such as Haverford, and in southern colleges and universities such as the University of Virginia and William and Mary. Other campuses adapted the honor code legacy into policies and conduct codes that were more heavily monitored by administration. These new approaches persisted into the contemporary university era.

The Contemporary University: 1975 to the Present

The seventies through the early nineties were marked by troubled financial times for colleges and universities caused by decreases in public funding. These financial difficulties along with a shift toward "universal access" led to what some refer to as the commercialization of postsecondary education (Slaughter and Leslie, 1997; Slaughter and Rhoades, 2004; Thelin, 2004).

Commercialization was marked by increased competition for private external funding and the enrollment of top students as well as increases in tuition. This commercialization led not just to greater public interest and scrutiny of post-secondary education and its management but also to students' and parents' believing their monetary contributions meant that colleges and universities had to meet their desires and demands (Thelin, 2004).

Competition among students for limited financial aid and graduate and medical school admittances became a well-known characteristic of postsecondary education institutions during this time. In his book *Campus Shock,* Lamont (1979) reported that students did not stop at old-fashioned cheating behaviors such as cribbing and copying. The overly competitive environment led students to steal books and examinations and to rip pages out of library books and jour-nals to secure an advantage over competing students. Students attempting to secure limited spots in professional or graduate schools hired exam takers and submitted "bogus transcripts or letters of recommendation" (Wentworth, 1976). This sort of cutthroat cheating seems rather unique to the 1970s, compared with the more cooperative cheating common in the latter part of the contemporary university era (Bertram Gallant, 2007). In cooperative cheating, students attempt to help themselves while helping others through the sharing of resources (such as old papers, lab reports, and examinations), divvying up the work required on assignments, and working together on independent assignments.

The spread of the Internet and the infusion of technology on college campuses has also been cited as a major contemporary force shaping students' academic conduct, faculty roles, and organizational responses to academic integrity (Maruca; 2005; Townley and Parsell, 2004; Ward, 2003). The moral panic surrounding student cheating intensified significantly toward the end of the twentieth century as online capabilities expanded and the use of the Internet proliferated among students. Colleges and universities began to rec-ognize that the Internet provided increased opportunities and resources for students' academic misconduct; students could easily copy material from any available source and paste it into their own papers. In addition, the term paper industry of the previous era boomed once it could be digitized and made avail-able online (type "free college essays" into a search engine for a demonstration of this resource explosion).

A Carnegie Council report in 1979 on fair practice for postsecondary institutions, however, suggested that it was the increasing pressures on postsecondary education organizations that led to unfair practices and the undermining of institutional integrity. Recent UNESCO reports echo the warnings of the Carnegie Council (Eckstein, 2003; Hallak and Poisson, 2007). Hallak and Poisson (2007) reveal that competition, organizational complexity, academic commercialization, and the far-reaching extent of the educational system have led to systemic and pervasive corruption of institutional integrity around the world. Faculty, for example, have been found to engage in questionable research practices and neglect their teaching duties because they are under pressure to publish and bring in revenue to the institution in the form of grants, donations, and commercialization of research end products (Braxton and Bayer, 1999, 2004; Hook, Kurtz, and Todorovich, 1977; Louis, Anderson, and Rosenberg, 1995; Rich, 1984; Scriven, 1982; Shils, 1978, 1983). Administrators, under pressure for funding, have been reported to fake enrollment numbers (Anglen, 2006).

The contemporary university era is thus marked by increasing calls for conduct codes and behavioral regulations for all members of the academy, not simply for students. For instance, both the NIH and the NSF began to require funded postsecondary institutions to implement policies, regulate researchers' behavior, and address research misconduct when it occurs (Fox and Braxton, 1994; Goodstein, 1991). Braxton and Bayer (2004) reinvigorated earlier calls for codes of conduct to guide teaching to ensure a "parallel infrastructure" to that found in research that will protect students' welfare and learning (p. 47). Colleges and universities have harnessed the power of technology to combat academic misconduct by regularly employing plagiarism detection software to detect and punish student plagiarism (Maruca, 2005). The sense of urgency surrounding issues of ethics and integrity seemed paramount during this era, most likely fueled in part by the capabilities of technology and public fascination with ethical scandals in the business and political worlds.

Misconduct Defined

By the contemporary university era, academic misconduct or cheating had come to represent any behaviors that were not authorized by the instructor, institution, or other authorities such as literary reference guides. The first mention of unauthorized collaboration (a quite common vernacular in the contemporary discourse on student academic misconduct) appeared during this era in a 1976 *Los Angeles Times* article entitled "Student Cheaters—They Crave Success." In that article, Occidental College's vice president was cited as saying "in-class exam cheating is not [my] major problem. . . . Students who copy research out of books without credit, improper footnotes, unauthorized 'teamwork' on research" are all more prevalent (Morrison, 1976). The definition of "cheating," then, expanded with both the expanding student population and the expanding popularity of methods for completing academic work. It may have been a natural shift as the institution of postsecondary education itself changed, becoming more complex and competitive (Eckstein, 2003).

Organizational Approaches

The idea of academic integrity, honor, or modified honor codes as a solution to students' cheating was reinvigorated in the 1990s as a result of the continued problem of student cheating, a flood of research conducted, the increasing call for codes of conduct for faculty and researchers, and influential writings by McCabe of Rutgers University and Pavela of the University of Maryland (Collison, 1990; McCabe and Pavela, 2000; Wilson, 1999). The contemporary honor code is "characterized by unproctored exams, a signed pledge, use of a peer judiciary and a duty to report" (Bush, 2000, p. 28). McCabe and Pavela (2000), however, suggest that the majority of schools should consider implementing a modified honor code that highlights an honor pledge, signing ceremonies, and student-run honor councils but may not include unproctored examinations or the obligation to report.

Lessons Learned

The history of academic integrity in the American academy demonstrates that the misconduct of students in their academic work is a perennial problem that survives the annual reconfiguration of the student body. Much can be learned from this historical review that can be applied to a more robust understanding of academic integrity in the twenty-first century and the development of a strategy to address the issue as a teaching and learning imperative.

A Narrowing of Academic Integrity

It was not until the latter half of the twentieth century that academic integrity came to be used synonymously (and almost exclusively) with student integrity. Before then, academic integrity appeared infrequently in either the popular or the scholarly press, but when it did, it usually referred more broadly to institutional integrity. The narrowing to student academic integrity may have been partly shaped by the appeal of the honor code that transferred responsibility for academic integrity from the faculty to students, but the lessons of the mass education era hint that misconduct by students and faculty (especially as researchers) is connected and simultaneously shaped by organizational, institutional, and societal forces. Thus it may be ineffectual to conceive of academic integrity as simply about students' academic conduct. Adopting a broader meaning of academic integrity as institutional integrity, on the other hand, may help campuses move the conversation from stopping students from cheating to ensuring that students are learning.

Waxing and Waning Concerns

The attention paid to academic misconduct by the public and the academic community has waxed and waned over time, usually spiking in response to cheating crises or to the introduction of technological or pedagogical innovations. Maruca (2005) has made this argument, connecting the contemporary "plagiarism panic" to the capabilities of the Internet. The modulating concern with academic integrity over time suggests that the issue and corresponding organizational responses are shaped by forces beyond the conduct of the individual student, faculty, researcher, or administrator. These forces originate from the organizational, institutional, and societal dimensions. Regardless of the reasons for modulating concerns, the change in public perception from amusement to moral panic over the last century is worth noting (Hart and Graham, n.d.; Maruca, 2005). It does not mean the current moral panic should not be responded to; however, panicked responses can be tempered by the understanding that bursts of panic have occurred throughout the history of postsecondary education.

Appearance of Increased Student Academic Misconduct

It is questionable whether academic misconduct is any more prevalent today than it was at any other point in history. It appears that cheating has always been perceived as a problem in colleges and universities, although as the student population grew and diversified, tolerance of academic misconduct as simple adolescent misbehavior weakened and institutions began to experience a moral panic around the perception of a cheating culture in the student body. The growing perception of a cheating culture may also be fueled by media coverage of the topic, increased access to cheating resources (through technology), and the expanding definition of student academic misconduct beyond copying or cribbing in examinations to unauthorized collaboration, homework copying, plagiarism, and fraud.

Certainly academic misconduct may be more visible because the number of students is greater and the expansion of academic integrity policies and procedures may have led to increased reporting. But whether the average twenty-first-century student cheats more or is less honorable than the average twentieth-century student cannot be said with certainty. Research studies that measure the extent of students' cheating must be carefully compared with previous studies before accurate comparisons over time can be made. For instance, McCabe's surveys of more than seventy thousand students in the United States and Canada since the early 1990s do not show evidence of a significant increase in misconduct since Bowers conducted his study in 1964 (McCabe, 2005a; McCabe and Bowers, 1994). As noted earlier, however, such comparisons have to be tenuously offered, given concerns about validity and reliability associated with survey research (Burrus, McGoldrick, and Schuhmann, 2007).

Academic Misconduct as Connected to Context

The historical review reveals that definitions and meanings of academic misconduct are dynamically shaped by context and events. Academic misconduct has been as specifically defined as cribbing on examinations and as broadly defined as any behaviors that are not authorized by the instructor. Moreover, the definitions adopted seem dependent on the contextual concerns at the time. For example, the rise of paper mills in the seventies and the Internet in the twenty-first century have both enhanced concerns with plagiarism and copying.

Thus, aspects beyond student character, including assessment methods, pedagogy, class sizes, and environmental pressures (such as graduate school competition), have all shaped definitions of and approaches to academic integrity. Changes in context and assessment methods challenge traditional notions of legitimate academic conduct. Proactive stances to such challenges rather than reactive stances to student behaviors may generate more intentional organizational strategies.

Effect of Student and Teacher Relations on Conduct

The ethical conduct of students, teachers, researchers, and administrators has historically been treated as discrete events disconnected from one another. The student affairs professional emerged to take over responsibility for student conduct from faculty, and separate offices (for example, research integrity, business affairs) were created to handle employee ethics and conflicts of interests. Yet the historical review suggests that at the very least the conduct of students and teachers should be considered in tandem. As early as the antebellum period, student cheating was thought to originate out of the adversarial relationship between student and teacher (Chipman and McDonald, 1982). More recently it has been posited that teaching misconduct can negatively affect student learning (Braxton and Bayer, 2004). Contemporary organizational approaches to student academic misconduct may then need to include attention to faculty conduct, at least in the arena most directly observed by students—the classroom.

Legacy of the Honor Code

Although it is debatable whether students are cheating more than in the past, it does seem that student academic misconduct is a normative behavior in the contemporary educational institution. In response, institutions of postsecondary education have reinvigorated the southern honor code tradition. Contemporary organizational approaches to student academic misconduct include the implementation of academic integrity policies, honor codes, or modified honor codes, and they are being implemented en masse. Bertram Gallant and Drinan (2006) found that 91 percent of surveyed institutions have some sort of integrity or dishonesty policy in place to address student academic misconduct. Aaron (1992) found a similar consistency across colleges and universities.

Despite organizational attempts to counter student academic practices, academic misconduct continues even in honor code schools (McCabe, Trevino, and Butterfield, 1999)—likely because integrity policies and honor codes "have never been quite successful in persuading young people that it is honorable to inform on their fellow students who have committed infractions" (Bowman, 2006, p. 5). The honor code legacy of conflicts between peer and institutional loyalties, then, persists in contemporary organizational approaches to academic misconduct (Drinan, 1999). These organizational approaches are explored in the next section.

Contemporary Organizational Strategies: Stopping Student Cheating

With more than half of Canadian university students cheating, all degrees are tainted. It's a national scandal. Why aren't schools doing more about it?

[University Fraud, 2007, front cover]

A PERCEPTION EXISTS that student cheating is out of control and that postsecondary education campuses, whether in Canada or the United States, are not doing enough to stop students from cheating. The contemporary moral panic over a cheating culture partly stems from a belief that the "rules of the game . . . [are] simple and uncontroversial: it is immoral for any student to present another's work as if it were his or her own or to assist another in doing so" (Hoekema, 1990, p. 187).

The historical review in the previous chapter, however, illuminated that student academic misconduct is indigenous to postsecondary education institutions, perhaps indicating that the rules are neither simple nor uncontroversial. In a competitive, hierarchical environment filled with young adults who believe that the success of their future depends on their ability to survive in that environment, behaviors that bend the norms or constitute blatant misconduct should not be surprising. This conclusion seems especially inevitable given that norms for academic conduct may be a moving target and the numbers of students competing in postsecondary education continue to substantially increase every few years.

What are schools doing about student academic misconduct in the twenty-first century? As will be shown in this section, campuses are legislating honor codes, modified honor codes, or academic integrity policies en masse under one of two strategies to curb student cheating. These two strategies—rule compliance and integrity—are the focus of this section.

A Comparison of the Strategies

An examination of the literature as well as institutional policies and processes suggests that when postsecondary education institutions intentionally respond to student academic misconduct, their responses trend toward two main organizational strategies—rule compliance and integrity (Paine, 1994; Whitley and Keith-Spiegel, 2002). The rule compliance strategy "emphasizes the establishment and enforcement of rules for behavior" (Whitley and Keith-Spiegel, 2002, p. 147), whereas the integrity strategy "seeks to enable responsible conduct" (Paine, 1994, p. 111). These strategies, however, have some common foundations because their origins are in the honor code legacy of American postsecondary education.

One common foundation of the two strategies is subscribing the cause of the problem to the character of the individual student actor, who is assumed to be dysfunctional or acting in dysfunctional ways. The strategy vernacular is morally laden, characterizing the actor and his or her conduct as honest or dishonest, honorable or dishonorable, moral or immoral, good or bad. In other words, behaviors considered to be misconduct are most commonly classified as "academic dishonesty" or "ethical transgressions," whether the conduct originates from ignorance or malice (Howard, 2000a, p. 82). Correspondingly, both strategies focus on resolving the problem primarily by addressing the student and preventing and punishing his or her misconduct.

The two strategies differ, however, in goals, method, and tone. In the rule compliance strategy, the goal is to create an environment in which students comply with institutional, departmental, and faculty rules. The method is predominantly disciplinarian, characterized by harsh sanctions such as suspension or dismissal (even for first offenses). Few developmental or pedagogical methods are used to reach the goal of rule compliance. The rule compliance strategy can be recognized by a tone of legality with use of words such as "theft," "fraud," "forgery," "misrepresentation," and "fabrication." A rule compliance strategy is often, but not always, marked by the use of lawyers either directly in an adjudication process or as consultants to the adjudicative bodies (that is, hearing boards).

In the integrity strategy, the method is predominantly developmental, characterized by sanctions and procedures that aim to reform the character of individual students. Discipline is still used to reinforce the integrity message, and pedagogical methods may extend to the implementation of ethics across the curriculum. The tone of the integrity strategy is strongly oriented toward forgiveness and second chances. Hoekema (1994), who surveyed chief student life officers at seventy-six U.S. colleges and universities, distinguishes between the rule compliance (punitive) and integrity (honor) strategies in this way: the rule compliance strategies "state that plagiarism and academic dishonesty are strictly prohibited and that violations of the policy will be dealt with severely," while the integrity strategies address the issue of honesty "by a comprehensive honor code to which all students are expected to subscribe" (p. 74).

Rule Compliance Strategy

In this strategy, academic conduct policies are traditionally included in the more general student conduct code that explicates the regulations to which students are expected to comply as well as the disciplinary processes that are applied when the policy is violated. The University of California system, for example, has one master document entitled *University of California Policies Applying to Campus Activities, Organizations and Students* from which individual campus policies guiding students' conduct are derived. At the University of California, Santa Barbara (UCSB), academic conduct is included under student conduct and discipline: "It is expected that students attending the University of California understand and subscribe to the ideal of academic integrity, and are willing to bear individual responsibility for their work. Any work (written or otherwise) submitted to fulfill an academic requirement must represent a student's original work. Any act of academic dishonesty, such as cheating or plagiarism, will subject a person to University disciplinary action" (University of California, Santa Barbara, 2005, par. 2).

After the first mention of academic integrity in the UCSB policy, the remaining document focuses on undesirable behaviors. Rule compliance policies tend to offer limited explanations of the meaning or importance of "individual responsibility" or "original work" but rather excessively expound on disciplinary matters such as procedural due process, disciplinary hearing bodies, disciplinary authority of faculty, and violations and sanctions. The UCSB policy is one illustration of the judicial stance common in the rule compliance strategy, which is "one of firm exhortation coupled with concern to instill an understanding of the nature and severity of the offense" (Hoekema, 1994, p. 78).

This rule compliance strategy, certainly not restricted to UC campuses, has three main characteristics. First, student academic conduct is treated primarily as a disciplinary issue and less as an issue of development or pedagogy (Michaels and Miethe, 1989). As a disciplinary issue, the focus is on ensuring that the costs of engaging in undesirable behaviors are higher than the rewards. Students who engage in misconduct are generally perceived as deviant, taking advantage of the institution and opportunities for cheating. Mechanisms for punishing rule violators are considered to be the most effective deterrents (Dalton, 1998).

The rule compliance strategy gained popularity in the late 1980s to early 1990s because of the perceived negative consequences of student misconduct (that is, threats to institutional reputation, public confrontation, and lawsuits) and the corresponding desire to regulate student behavior (Dannells, 1997; Hoekema, 1994; Michaels and Miethe, 1989). Thus, the second common characteristic of the rule compliance strategy is the management of policy and processes by judicial affairs or other student affairs administrators rather than by students or faculty themselves. This transfer of responsibility for academic integrity from the hands of the students and faculty into those of student affairs administrators is considered necessary as campuses move to suspend or dismiss students for academic misconduct: "As campus experts on student rights and responsibilities, student affairs administrators must assume their full measure of responsibility for maintaining academic integrity" (Hall and Kuh, 1998, p. 14).

Hoekema (1994), after a study of campus rules through survey and document analysis, also argued the necessity of this shift from faculty to administrators because "the task of countering improper behavior has become more complex, as student rights to privacy and autonomy have come to be more generally recognized" (p. 61). As illuminated in the historical review, the meaning of academic integrity narrowed over time from institutional integrity to student academic integrity. This narrowing could have been partly fueled by the shifting of responsibility for academic integrity from the faculty and students in the classroom to the student affairs professional, whose primary focus is on students and student life.

Thus, the third common characteristic of the rule compliance strategy is that its underlying purpose is to regulate or control student behavior in a way that complies with institutional rules (Dalton, 1998). Under the rule compliance strategy student academic misconduct is approached in the same way as other forms of undesirable student behaviors such as drinking, noise violations, and student protests. Although student protests may seem an unlikely fit, the University of California provides a specific example of the way in which the rule compliance strategy serves to regulate and control students' conduct. The University of California, San Diego, document *Free Speech: How to Express Your Message* informs students of the designated "free speech" areas, protest restrictions (such as the use of pickets), and the disciplinary procedures to which they will be held accountable if they violate these conduct rules. Any behaviors seen as a threat to the welfare of the institution and its organizational members, then, are collapsed into a general definition of misconduct and controlled by the explication and enforcement of rules.

The rule compliance strategy seems to be most prevalent in large institutions and those with a significant research focus, likely because it is an easier strategy to apply when faculty-student ratios are high and the judicial affairs office is adequately staffed. The rule compliance strategy tends to lead to an overly legalistic process for handling student academic misconduct, an approach that actually may be unnecessary (Buchanan and Beckham, 2006). The courts allow educational organizations to distinguish between academic and nonacademic offenses and to sanction academic offenses in the normal processes of "academic decision making" (Mawdsley, 1994, p. 51). At the most basic level, students must be afforded "due process"; that is, they must be provided with notice and an opportunity to be heard by those with the expertise and skills to come to a fair and unbiased judgment (Buchanan and Beckham, 2006;

Hardy and Burch, 1981; Mawdsley, 1994). Despite being superfluous, elaborate bureaucracies to prevent, police, and punish student academic misconduct are commonplace in institutions employing the rule compliance strategy.

Integrity Strategy

Proponents of the integrity strategy generally accept the principle that "colleges and universities have a responsibility for . . . the moral principles and attitudes of the young people under their charge" (Schnepp, 1940, p. 81). The international Center for Academic Integrity strongly supports the integrity strategy, which reinforces the moral and ethical dimensions of academic conduct through its publications (such as *The Fundamental Values of Academic Integrity),* conferences, and research support (for example, the Templeton research program, which examines the ties between student academic conduct and moral development). The following quote from a book for new college students exemplifies the tenor of the integrity strategy: "The college-trained should be leaders in moral behavior as well as scholarship. They have had the advantage of acquiring the American traditions of freedom, integrity, democracy, tolerance, and honesty. They should demand of themselves goodness and integrity. . . . A society [that] grants the privilege of much training to a select group of its members has a right to expect a high level of moral integrity of them, for they are to be its leaders" (Landis, 1954, p. 178).

Under the integrity strategy, probably more common in liberal arts or teaching-centered institutions, student academic misconduct is assumed to result from underdeveloped moral or ethical reasoning as well the students' inability to understand the importance of integrity in their academic work (Bush, 2000; Dalton, 1998; Dannells, 1997). In accordance with this underlying belief, integrity strategy policies usually take the form of honor or modified honor codes that put "policing academic dishonesty" in the background and . . . "teaching values of honesty and integrity" in the foreground (McCabe, 1993, p. 657). The integrity strategy includes the disciplinary method for responding to academic misconduct but not as the primary method. Rather disciplinary and developmental methods are both included as "part of the educational process" (Dannells, 1997, p. xii).

The integrity strategy emerged most forcefully in the 1990s with "the burgeoning growth of developmental theory, concurrent with our disenchantment with 'legalism' over the last 20 or so years" (Dannells, 1997, p. 93). Kibler did much to advocate the application of student developmental theory to resolve the problem of academic misconduct (Kibler, 1993a, 1993b, 1994; Kibler, Nuss, Paterson, and Pavela, 1988). Student developmental theory suggests that student "cheating" can best be reduced if educational institutions develop in students the moral and ethical compass that will direct them to "adopt the fundamental values associated with good scholarship and embrace the standards of academic integrity" and "respond to ethical dilemmas" accordingly (Kibler, 1993a, p. 263). The goal of the integrity strategy, then, is to reform (through discipline and remediation) rather than remove individual students from campus.

Another central feature of the integrity strategy is the continuous focus on communicating "to students the importance of academic integrity as a core institutional value" (McCabe and Pavela, 2000, p. 35). The integrity strategy usually involves faculty, students, and staff on honor councils (who decide on cases and sanctions) as well as in seminars, discussions, and presentations on ethics, honesty, and integrity. Advocates of the integrity strategy categorically see "academic dishonesty [as] a moral development problem" and strongly argue that "tempering sanctions with moral education may be the best response that institutions could offer to those students found guilty of such misconduct" (Bush, 2000, p. 96).

The honor system at Kansas State University (KSU) is an exemplary approach of the integrity strategy to student academic misconduct in a large research institution. KSU's honor system (www.k-state.edu/honor) is fundamentally different from the rule compliance approach in three main ways: (1) academic integrity is managed separately from nonacademic misconduct (for example, it is not housed under judicial affairs); (2) students play a significant role in adjudication and education; and (3) the commonly applied sanction is an academic integrity seminar. At Kansas State, for example, most students found responsible for academic misconduct are required to take a development and integrity course taught through the university's College of Education. The course syllabus illustrates the essence of the integrity strategy:

The . . . course is a general overview of ethics and ethical decision making in academia and professional life. The course initiates students in college student development theory, especially moral judgment (reasoning) development as espoused by Arthur Chickering, Lawrence Kohlberg, Carol Gilligan, and James Rest. Texts, cases, videos, the worldwide web, and handouts are all used to help students better understand several approaches to ethical decision-making— principles-based, case-based, virtues-based, and responsibility-based. The course further instructs students in developing the rationale and skills for better decision making when confronted with dilemmas. Students are taught a framework for regular moral reflection, and then are encouraged to teach others [Marcoux, 2001].

The purpose of sanctioning in the integrity strategy is to reform the individual student in a way that develops his or her ethical reasoning and moral judgment. This approach acknowledges that institutional forces such as grades and pressures create ethical dilemmas for students but conceives of student misconduct as primarily a result of the student's inability to make the right choice when facing these dilemmas. The KSU Web site and corresponding materials are typical of the integrity strategy, which, according to Hoekema (1994), tend to be "more formal and categorical" (p. 79) about the importance of honor and honesty "to create a moral atmosphere" (p. 78) on campus. This "moral atmosphere" is thought to be created by the clarification of "cheating" as a "moral choice—that there is a clear right and wrong and that any form of cheating is morally wrong and cannot be justified by situational constraints" (Eisenberg, 2004, p. 176).

Summary

Although the rule compliance and integrity strategies are primarily focused on changing students and controlling their conduct, the focus, tone, and framing of the approaches are distinct (see Exhibit 1). Questions of pedagogy and questions of faculty and administrator conduct can emerge from these strategies, but they tend to revolve around how faculty and administrators can stop

EXHIBIT 1
Summary Comparison of the Rule Compliance and Integrity Strategies

	Rule Compliance	*Stopping Students from Cheating*	*Integrity*

Characterization of the Problem or Issue

Rule Compliance	*Integrity*
Academic misconduct is considered primarily a judicial issue along with other student conduct problems, such as alcohol use and social disobedience.	Academic integrity is primarily considered an area to be developed along with moral citizenship and ethical leadership.

Characterization of the Students

Rule Compliance	*Integrity*
Students are doing bad things that harm themselves, others, and the environment and thus they must be stopped.	Students are making poor choices from which they need to learn through punishment and ethics education or moral development.

Characterization of the Solution

Rule Compliance	*Integrity*
Academic misconduct can be controlled by disciplining students, consistently enforcing the rules, and removing offending students from the institution.	Academic integrity can be enhanced by educating students, communicating the importance of integrity, and enrolling offending students in ethics or integrity seminars.

Common Strategy Questions

Rule Compliance	*Integrity*
How are students violating institutional rules?	Why do students violate institutional rules?
How do we get students to comply with our rules?	How can we reform students?
How do we encourage faculty to report students so we can catch repeat offenders?	How do we create cultures of integrity in which integrity is normative?

(continued)

EXHIBIT 1 (*continued*)
Summary Comparison of the Rule Compliance and Integrity Strategies

Stopping Students from Cheating	
Rule Compliance	*Integrity*
Primary Organizational Actions	
Encourage faculty to devise mechanisms to make cheating difficult	Facilitate moral development (after misconduct has occurred)
Implement punishments to increase the cost of cheating	Implement ethical interventions and programs, such as ethics across the curriculum
Decrease costs to faculty for enforcing rules and reporting students	Create second chances and opportunities for learning from mistakes
Espouse that students are trusted to comply with rules and be honest in their academic work	Espouse that students are expected to live, study, and work with integrity and honor
Course syllabi are typically absent of much detail on academic conduct, but might simply say "students are expected to comply with institutional policies on academic integrity."	Course syllabi typically include detailed information about course expectations, including perhaps an honor pledge or code for students to sign, for example, "on my honor, I . . ."
Common Organizational Structures	
Student conduct code that covers academic misconduct	A specific academic integrity policy, modified honor code, or honor code (may also still be under general conduct code)
Judicial affairs officers and a judicial court system to handle academic violations	Administrators generally handle academic violations, but may be under student or academic affairs (depending on the institution).
Students are seldom involved in enforcement.	Students are heavily involved in honor codes.

student academic misconduct and teach students how to be better behaved, morally developed, and responsible citizens (see Exhibit 2). The framing of these approaches limits the consideration of students as offenders rather than learners and faculty as parole officers rather than as teachers. Bayer (2004) also noted this limitation in his examination of integrity policies: "perhaps most remarkable in a perusal of institutional publications on student conduct is the general lack of specification of improper conduct in the student-as-learner role. Most codes refer to prohibition of plagiarism and cheating; but most codes go little beyond these proscribed acts to other student [and faculty] behaviors relative to the [teaching and] learning environment" (p. 82).

In fact, both strategies place the primary responsibility for enhancing and upholding the integrity of the institution in the actions of the student body, rather than in the actions of faculty, staff, administrators, or the institution as a whole. For example:

> The University is an academic community. Its fundamental purpose is the pursuit of knowledge. Like all other communities, the University can function properly only if its members adhere to clearly established goals and values. Essential to the fundamental purpose of the University is the commitment to the principles of truth and academic honesty. Accordingly, The Code of Academic Integrity is designed to ensure that the principle of academic honesty is upheld. While all members of the University share this responsibility, The Code of Academic Integrity is designed so that special responsibility for upholding the principle of academic honesty lies with the students [University of Maryland, 2005, par. 1].

Although the code begins with an acknowledgment that all members of the university share the responsibility for upholding the principle of academic honesty, the code ends with a reaffirmation of the primary responsibility residing in the student body.

Generally, the rule compliance strategy, characterized as "faculty/administrator centered," is more commonly adopted in the contemporary postsecondary education institution than is the integrity strategy, characterized as

EXHIBIT 2
Dominant Organizational Strategies for Stopping Students From Cheating

Techniques (for achieving the strategy)	Strategies	
	Rule-Compliance	Integrity
	Focus is on ensuring that students comply with the rules for academic conduct; not much concern with changing cultures or organizations, just controlling behavior	Focus is on the integrity or honor of the individual student and student body at large; changing the student subculture (that is, from "dishonest" to "honest")
Discipline	Achieving compliance with academic conduct rules through a focus on policy, procedures, and swift disciplinary actions. The school spends a significant amount of space and time explaining rules and focusing on due process, but the goal is to "rid" the institution of (rather than reform) the offender, thereby affecting the actions of others.	Instilling integrity or honor by instituting an honor code that is strictly enforced by a student-majority honor council (see the Air Force Academy for an example). Discipline is used as a consequence for violating the honor code and is a "mark" on one's own integrity.
Development	Achieving compliance through a focus on developing students' ethical and moral reasoning so that they see rule compliance as morally right and, when they don't, accept responsibility for their actions and learn from their mistakes	Instilling integrity or honor by developing students as "moral citizens"—usually the approach to academic integrity is tied to a broader citizenship initiative within the institution. A moral development course for integrity violators is standard.
Pedagogy	A seldom-used technique for the rule compliance strategy. When implemented, predominantly used in response to plagiarism—achieving compliance through teaching students about the rules (for example, citation and attribution) and offering research-writing classes to teach source citation and attribution technique.	Ethics across the curriculum is one technique in the integrity strategy, as are workshops, presentations, guest speakers, summer reading programs, and so on, all centered on the theme of developing "personal integrity" or "professional ethics".

student centered (Bush, 2000). The purest form of the integrity strategy, the honor code, is the least typical because it eliminates examination proctoring and requires students to report misconduct. Thus, the honor code is most prevalent in "private schools with small to moderate enrollments" (McCabe and Pavela, 2000, p. 34). The most common form of the integrity strategy is the modified honor code, which heavily involves students in enforcement and adjudication but does not place control fully in their hands. Large research institutions that adopt an integrity strategy, like Kansas State University, are more likely to adopt the modified honor code or an academic integrity policy rather than the traditional honor code.

Although an honor code is not synonymous with the integrity strategy, an honor code is usually a symbol that the integrity strategy rather than the rule compliance strategy has been adopted. If it is true, available data suggest that the rule compliance strategy is more commonly employed by colleges and universities than is the integrity strategy. The CAI reports that only 270 colleges and universities currently employ an integrity strategy (represented by an honor or modified honor code) over the traditional rule compliance (that is, judicial) strategy. Bush (2000), in his survey study of 132 CAI institutional members, found that fewer than half the institutions employed an integrity strategy.

Although the rule compliance and integrity strategies are both attractive and practical to apply, their effectiveness has not been proved at any point in the history of postsecondary education. As indicated, researchers and writers have questioned the effectiveness of honor codes and honor systems throughout the twentieth century (Drake, 1941; Hall and Kuh, 1998; Matthews, 1932). And even the most adamant contemporary advocates have cautioned against the use of conduct codes as a panacea (Bowers, 1964; Bush, 2000; Hall and Kuh, 1998; McCabe and Trevino, 1993, 1997). Many argue that the size and complexity of the student body as well as the disparate notions of honor and integrity limit the potential of conduct codes to control student academic behaviors (Angell, 1928; Drake, 1941; Middlebrook, 1961; Trombley, 1965). Cheating scandals at those institutions revered for their honor codes and sense of honor (such as the University of Virginia, the Air Force Academy, and Princeton) have contributed to concerns about the effectiveness of codes (Schemo, 2001).

Why, then, has the conduct code not only persevered throughout time but continued to be implemented and shored with additional rules and integrity statements? As the next section demonstrates, the research conducted on misconduct in the academy may be partly responsible for the endurance of the conduct code approach. For the better half of the twentieth century, the majority of the research explained academic misconduct as a result of the internal characteristics, traits, and motivations of students. Even with evidence that suggests multidimensionality, research on this internal dimension of academic misconduct continues to exert a powerful influence to the extent that the organizational, institutional, and societal dimensions are recognized less often or with less intensity.

Dimensions of the Issue: Toward a Robust Explanation

A S ILLUSTRATED IN THE PREVIOUS SECTION, contemporary postsecondary educational institutions trend toward one of two strategies to address academic misconduct: rule compliance or integrity. Both these strategies favor a microlevel explanation of the problem; that is, academic integrity is undermined by dishonest students and their cheating behaviors. The historical overview, however, noted that the issue is not one dimensional but multidimensional. To explore this implication, the research on academic misconduct is analyzed and thematically coded. A four-dimensional picture of academic misconduct is the result.

This section explores these four dimensions—internal, organizational, institutional, and societal—that shape the academic misconduct problem in postsecondary education. The intent of presenting the multidimensional nature of academic misconduct is twofold. First, I demonstrate that no dimension by itself can explain academic misconduct. Microexplanations (at the internal level) ignore the relationships and contexts that shape agency actions. Mesoexplanations (at the organizational and institutional levels) downplay the internal aspect and ignore the larger system factors that exert force on the issue. And, finally, macroexplanations (at the societal level) dangerously tread on a relativist position that negates the power and accountability of actors, organizations, and institutions to modify their behaviors and situations. Thus, although presented here separately, the four dimensions together create a lens through which the problem can be viewed and robust possibilities explored.

Second, I further the argument that the predominant organizational strategies are limited because they do not take into account the multidimensional nature of academic misconduct. Tensions in the strategies as well as forces acting on student and faculty actors are revealed through the multidimensional lens. I argue in a later chapter that the acceptance of the multidimensional nature of academic misconduct requires a new organizational strategy that focuses on teaching and learning.

The Four Dimensions

A review of the research and the literature suggests that academic misconduct has at least four dimensions (see Figure 1). At the center of the four dimensional lens is the internal dimension—the character, traits, motivations, and so on of the individual actor. The internal dimension has been the most thoroughly examined and explained over the years, most likely because one of the core responsibilities of postsecondary education has been to develop the character and "intellectual curiosity" of its students (Angell, 1928; Bok, 1990; Briggs, 1969; Landis, 1954; McBee, 1978; Thelin, 2004). At this microlevel, academic misconduct is theorized to be a result of individual dysfunction in

FIGURE 1
The Four Dimensions of Academic Misconduct

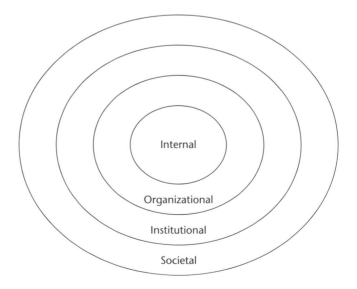

which an actor's internal ethical barometer is off a few degrees from organizational, institutional, or societal ethical barometers.

The next level is the organizational dimension—the culture and immediate context in which the student actor lives and study. The research on this mesodimension predominantly explores social norms in educational organizational subcultures and the influence of organizational artifacts and values on the actor's conduct (Alschuler and Blimling, 1995; Dalton, 1998; Davis, Grover, Becker, and McGregor, 1992; Kaplan and Mable, 1998; McCabe and Drinan, 1999; Payne and Nantz, 1994; Whitley and Keith-Spiegel, 2001, 2002; Wilcox and Ebbs, 1992). These mesolevel explanations posit academic misconduct as a result of a cheating culture; actors engage in behaviors that may constitute "cheating," but such behaviors are supported by cultural norms and values.

The next dimension is an extension of the organizational dimension to include the larger educational institution or academic systems of which individual organizations are a part. Research at this other mesodimension considers the ways in which educational system characteristics (such as structures, rules, and norms) shape academic conduct (Amsden, 1977; Barnes, 1975; Bunn, Caudill, and Gropper, 1992; David and Kovach, 1979; Hardy, 1982; Houston, 1976; McKenzie, 1979a, 1979b). Academic misconduct is explained as a natural by-product of a system that sets actors to compete against one another and rewards actors for prioritizing unethical actions over others.

The fourth dimension of academic misconduct is the societal dimension. This macrolevel explanation characterizes academic misconduct as a symptom of unresolved complex problems such as clashes between cultures or conflicts between competing interests or ideas. Individual actions are considered to be shaped by larger forces that transcend internal, organizational, and institutional boundaries such as power, authority, and privilege (Apple, 2003; Giroux, 1983; Howard, 1995, 2000a, 2000b; Lindey, 1952; Marsh, 2004; Maruca, 2001, 2003, 2005; McLaren, 1989).

Internal Dimension: Student Character

"Ethics involves one's moral principles and intellectual honesty . . . [and] the student who willfully plagiarizes thereby admits his lack of ethics. This weakness in ethical behavior can be partially attributed

to the student's lack of knowledge as to the purposes of footnotes and
the theory of scholarly documentation, as well as to a weakness in the
moral fiber of the individual" [Shurtleff, 1968, p. 94].

As evident in this quote, microlevel explanations focus on the internal dimension, suggesting that academic misconduct is a result of an individual's underdeveloped "moral fiber" or ethical barometer. The institutional rules governing academic conduct (such as citation and attribution) are considered to be moral absolutes by which honest, moral, and ethical people abide.

Parr's writing (1936) about "the problem of student honesty" is one of the earliest pieces found that reflect this internal perspective. After studying 409 college students over a two-year period, Parr concluded that "any factor [that] serves as a handicap to an individual . . . is likely to produce dishonest behavior" (p. 326). Parr found such handicaps to be age, mental ability, and grade point average. As a result of his findings, Parr suggested that student academic misconduct could best be addressed through "a character-training program [that] will focus attention on those individuals who are most likely to be tempted to deviate from proper conduct. If, during their early years, we can teach individuals to aspire to success in school or in life through honest means only, we will be making a long step toward training honest young men and women for the future" (p. 326). In summary, the internal dimension rests the problem and the solution of academic misconduct on the individual student; the problem is deviant behavior, and the solution is character and cognitive development.

Research and writings on the internal dimension continued to be prevalent throughout the twentieth and into the twenty-first century and further elucidated the qualities, traits, or dysfunctions that predispose students to engage in deviant behavior (see, for example, Covey, Saladin, and Killen, 2001; Diekhoff and others, 1996; Haines, Diekhoff, LaBeff, and Clark, 1986; Houston, 1983; Loofbourow and Keys, 1933; Steininger, Johnson, and Kirts, 1964; Ward, 2001). Such studies found that academic conduct is internally regulated by internal versus external orientation (Davis, Grover, Becker, and McGregor, 1992; Lewis and Hartnett, 1983); ethical orientation or development (Eisenberg, 2004; Houston, 1983; Kibler, 1993a; Malinowski and Smith, 1985; Pratt and McLaughlin, 1989); anxiety or hostility felt toward the teacher or situation

(Gerdeman, 2000; Steininger, Johnson, and Kirts, 1964); self-esteem (Ward, 2001); and low self-awareness (Malcolm and Ng, 2001).

This focus on discovering the internal characteristics that lead students to academic deviance may stem from the educational commitment to train moral citizens for society while simultaneously protecting the rule of order in the institution (Briggs, 1969; Landis, 1954; Pusey, 1978). According to Pusey (1978), the "whole person" approach to producing graduates with "moral probity" greatly shaped the educational system between 1945 to 1970 (p. 180). Undergraduates, as future leaders of society, are expected to maintain their integrity in the face of the pressures and stresses of postsecondary education (see, for example, Callahan, 2004; Dalton, 1998; Haines, Diekhoff, LaBeff, and Clark, 1986; Lamont, 1979). Even more strongly, however, the predominance of the internal dimension explanation can be tied to the private and autonomous nature of academic work; because the performance of academic work is often under the scrutiny of no one other than the involved person, only the involved person can ensure academic integrity. Angell (1928) suggested that no matter the faults of the institution, which he admits are many, "the chief blame . . . [lies] with the students themselves" (p. 214).

The fundamental premise of the internal dimension, then, is that the student who engages in academic misconduct is morally corrupt: he or she chooses behaviors that he or she knows to be deviant from the "right" ways of completing academic work. The internal dimension does not create a space for critique of the environment or other stakeholders or an assessment of the changing norms and expectations regarding the pursuit of truth or learning. More fundamentally, it neglects that research has failed to demonstrate a causal relationship between internal factors, moral development, and student academic misconduct (Beck and Ajzen, 1991; Brimble and Stevenson-Clarke, 2006; Park, 2003).

Organizational Dimension: Peer Norms and Classroom Dynamics

The essential argument in the organizational dimension is that the "campus climate or culture may be the most important determinant of the level of student cheating" (McCabe and Trevino, 1996, p. 30). The research at this mesolevel explanation delineates between two "levels" of campus climate—peer group and classroom (Alschuler and Blimling, 1995; Dalton, 1998; Davis, Grover, Becker, and McGregor, 1992; Kaplan and Mable, 1998; McCabe and Drinan, 1999; Payne and Nantz, 1994; Whitley and Keith-Spiegel, 2001, 2002; Wilcox and Ebbs, 1992). More specifically, research in the organizational dimension has demonstrated that student academic conduct is shaped by the (perceived or real) norms of the student subculture and classroom dynamics (Beck and Ajzen, 1991; Hard, Conway, and Moran, 2006; Jordan, 2001; Maller, 1932; McCabe, 2005b; McCabe and Trevino, 1993, 2002; Pratt and McLaughlin, 1989).

Peer Norms

Norms of the student subculture have been of particular interest among academic misconduct researchers (Bowers, 1964; Genereux and McLeod, 1995; Gerdeman, 2000; Hard, Conway, and Moran, 2006; McCabe and Trevino, 1993, 1997). The peer culture has been found to trump the organizational ethos so that "when there is a clash between institutional norms and peer-group norms, many students prefer to invest in their relationship with their peers . . . at the expense of violating school conduct codes" (Eisenberg, 2004, p. 174). Support for this phenomenon has been found in the earliest experimental studies. Maller (1932) found that students would be "dishonest" to help their peer group. Shaffer (1966) noted that "evidence continues to accumulate that cheating is both prevalent and widely tolerated in American education. Numerous student surveys and occasional cheating scandals support a popular impression that student honesty is at a low level. Perhaps most disturbing are indications that cheating is becoming an ingrained part of student life in the United States" (p. 343).

The first comprehensive study reflecting the organizational dimension of academic misconduct was published in 1960 by Goldsen, Rosenberg, Williams, and Suchman. *What College Students Think* was a massive survey of more than forty-five hundred students at various high-profile institutions (such as UCLA, Cornell, Michigan, Dartmouth, Yale, and Harvard). As a result of their study, Goldsen and his colleagues concluded that cheating (which they restricted to examination cribbing or copying) was directly related to actual or perceived normative behavior of peers, normative expectations or standards of the institution (represented by social controls), and the academic climate. Survey research has also shown, however, that peers often overestimate the extent to which other students engage in academic misconduct (Hard, Conway, and Moran, 2006; Jordan, 2001). This observation is important because peer descriptive norms have been shown to influence behavior in other areas such as binge drinking (Berkowitz, 2005), and it is likely that student descriptive norms about academic misconduct could have the same affect (Bowers, 1964; Genereux and McLeod, 1995; Gerdeman, 2000; Hard, Conway, and Moran, 2006; McCabe and Trevino, 1993, 1997).

Classroom Dynamics
Student academic conduct has historically, in practice and research, been considered in relation to other forms of student conduct (for example, underage drinking and social disturbances) and not in tandem with classroom dynamics. A handful of authors, however, have argued that student and faculty behaviors in the classroom (or in activities associated with the classroom such as grading or completion of homework assignments) are not isolated events but together interact to shape classroom climate (Boice, 1996; Braxton and Bayer, 1994; Faia, 1976; McBee, 1978; Parr, 1936; Pratt and McLaughlin, 1989; Puka, 2005; Rich, 1984; Shils, 1978; Wilson, 1982). "Classroom incivilities," including academic misconduct, undermine or directly "intrude into the student-faculty relationship in ways that are highly damaging" (Faia, 1976, p. 116), including the disruption of learning that may otherwise take place (Becker, Geer, and Hughes, 1968; Boice, 1996; Braxton and Bayer, 1999; Scriven, 1982).

Faculty shape classroom dynamics, decide what students get to learn, and teach values simply in the everyday act of teaching (Churchill, 1982; Gehring and Pavela, 1994; Markie, 1994; McCabe and Pavela, n.d.; Rudolph and Timm, 1998). Thus, classroom incivilities on the part of the teacher that affect student academic conduct can range from the mundane (unarticulated or ambiguous expectations) to the moderate (filibustering to kill class time) to the severe (condescending commentary that creates a hostile climate) (Faia, 1976;

Wilson 1982). Barnett and Dalton (1981), for instance, found that "the regular administration of 'old' tests can foster the belief among students that faculty don't care about academic integrity" (p. 550).

Research on the classroom climate suggests, then, that student academic misconduct might be greatly reduced if faculty paid more attention to their teaching and clearly expressed their conceptions of legitimate academic work, especially in those areas of misconduct where there is likely misunderstanding and confusion (such as authorship and collaboration). The reuse of old examinations by teachers may be particularly influential because students see this behavior as similar to their own choice to recycle a paper or use another student's lab report as a model for their own. Thus, a student's decision to complete his or her academic work in a certain way may in part be considered a legitimate way to respond to professorial behavior or unfair assessment methods (Introna, Hayes, Blair, and Wood, 2003; Roberts and Rabinowitz, 1992).

Institutional Dimension: Academic Systems

The institutional dimension of academic misconduct acknowledges that the educational institution is not an innocent bystander or victim of student academic misconduct but an active participant in the shaping of it (Amsden, 1977; Barnes, 1975; Bunn, Caudill, and Gropper, 1992; David and Kovach, 1979; Hardy, 1982; Houston, 1976; McKenzie, 1979a, 1979b). One institutional facet thought to shape student and faculty (as teacher and researcher) conduct is the competitive marketplace (Bok, 1990; Townley and Parsell, 2004). Faculty perceive a great and mounting pressure to publish and produce results for the institution that can be measured by a dollar figure, and students perceive a similar pressure to produce "perfect" pieces of academic work (Bertram Gallant, 2006). In particular, a focus on the transactional rather than transformational relationship between the students and the institution may shape the way in which students engage with their academic work—students pay money not to receive an education but to receive the credits necessary to move upward in society (Amsden, 1977; Bellico, 1979; David and Kovach, 1979). In essence, students pay for the opportunity to achieve the ends by whatever means necessary.

The impact of the grading system on student conduct is perhaps the most widely explored issue of the institutional dimension (Becker, Geer, and Hughes, 1968; Bowers, 1968; Drake, 1941; Houston, 1976). Drake (1941), who published one of the earliest studies of academic misconduct in college, noted that "it is evident cheating grows out of the competitive system under which college credits are awarded" (p. 420). Bowers (1968) also commented that grading systems are powerful shapers of student academic conduct because they are "a means to many important ends" (p. 77) such as employment and graduate education. As indicators of a student's intelligence, abilities, and potential, grades serve as a "kind of social credit" in social and work settings (Bowers, 1968, p. 77). Houston (1976) also concluded that grades may be the end to which student academic misconduct is oriented. In his experimental study, Houston found that students who were told their tests would not count toward the class grade did not engage in significant copying compared with the group for whom the tests would count.

In *Making the Grade,* Becker, Geer, and Hughes (1968) argue that student orientation toward the grade (rather than toward learning or scholarship) is an irrefutable part of the educational system that "constitute[s] the conditions under which the student builds his definition of the situation in which he pursues his academic work" (p. 45). In other words, the way in which the institution is set up shapes students' academic conduct. Students are thought to choose behaviors that the institution defines as academic misconduct because the institution actually rewards them for doing so: "the most important point about illegitimate actions is that they are a consequence of the existence of a system of examinations, grades, and grade point averages. If the faculty uses examinations and other assignments to evaluate the student's abilities or progress, some students will attempt to influence the outcome of the evaluation 'illegally,' by 'brown nosing,' arguing, or cheating. Illegitimate actions would be foolish if nothing important could be gained from them. It is because they may be rewarded by a raised grade that students engage in them" (Becker, Geer, and Hughes, 1968, pp. 101–102).

According to economic theory, people make rational choices based on their motivation to avoid or reduce expected costs and increase or enhance expected rewards; "cheating" occurs when the expected benefits of the chosen conduct exceed the expected costs (Beck and Ajzen, 1991; Hardy, 1982; McKenzie, 1979b; Passow and others, 2006). And the benefits of cheating may far outweigh the costs of not cheating in the current high-stakes testing environments common in contemporary educational institutions. Researchers and journalists have argued that No Child Left Behind in the United States or the 1988 Education Act in Britain, for example, encouraged teachers and administrators to artificially inflate students' standardized test scores and grades to meet policy requirements and expected results (Eckstein, 2003; Hoff, 2000; Keller, 2002).

The pressure for higher grades may be particularly influential on the student who lacks power or control over much of the transactional aspects of education—especially in large classes with standardized methods of testing and prescribed texts or modes of studying. Hardy (1982) argued this point: "because of ever-shrinking resources and a frequent paucity of adequate classroom facilities, many colleges and universities are forced to administer examinations in extremely crowded conditions. . . . Faced with the impersonal nature of the institution, a frequent lack of interest in the subject matter, and increasing academic demands, many students consider cheating as a way to solve their problems" (p. 69). Thus, the institutional dimension posits that when students perceive that instructors, coursework, difficult assignments, or other institutional constraints inhibit their chances for future successes, they will choose to engage in the behaviors necessary for them to succeed (David and Kovach, 1979; Hardy, 1982).

From this perspective, if there are not significant costs to cheating (for example, the likelihood of getting caught or harsh punishment), then students in environments focused on grades, competition, and large classes (that is, symbols of a cold transactional environment) will likely choose the most effective and efficient means for completing course requirements and earning a satisfactory grade. In some cases, the institution may label those chosen means as "cheating," but the student may not engage in them with the intent to "deceive." The existence of legalized institutional systems that provide legitimate academic assistance (such as coaching for standardized tests and term-paper writing services) may exacerbate the perception that grade achievement is more important than the learning process (Amsden, 1977; David and Kovach, 1979; Hardy, 1982).

Societal Dimension: Broader Societal Forces

Published pieces on the societal dimension of academic misconduct are few and far between, but the existing pieces focus commentary and arguments on the larger context beyond the individual student, the organization, and the educational institution to the society in which the students and institutions reside. It is in this societal context that changing norms and expectations for behaviors emerge and subsequently mold and shape the actions of individuals and institutions. Critical theorists, then, are the most predominant writers in the societal dimension. Critical education theorists suggest that contextual forces, power, authority, and privilege all contribute to the shaping of the actions of faculty, students, researchers, and administrators and the way in which their actions are perceived and defined by others (Apple, 2003; Giroux, 1983; McLaren, 1989; Tierney, 1991). Critical theorists deconstruct that which is normally taken for granted or commonly understood by those in power and authority, that is, within the dominant culture, to provide alternative perspectives that may inform social change.

Critical writers on academic integrity, then, question the assumptive stances taken by the institution, deconstruct definitions of academic misconduct, and critique the ways in which forces (such as technology) may be shaping academic conduct (Bertram Gallant, 2006; Howard, 1995, 2000a, 2000b; Lindey, 1952; Marsh, 2004; Maruca, 2001, 2003, 2005). Other than my own writings, these writings reside mainly in the fields of composition and instructional technology and focus on plagiarism and thus have yet to significantly inform the main body of research and practice on academic integrity. Mainstream writers have mentioned technology as a warning against the ease with which students can now "cheat" rather than as a starting point for critique.

Lindey's work (1952), *Plagiarism and Originality,* is perhaps one of the earliest pieces that describes the societal dimension. Although not specifically on student plagiarism, it is a critique of the concept of plagiarism as tied to notions of originality and authorship, which Lindey challenges as not necessarily representing a "badge of genius" (p. 14). Lindey's contribution is his contextualization of plagiarism in societal norms and technological forces, noting that the rising concerns with plagiarism are directly related to "the invention of the printing press and the rise of the concept of literary property," not in the perceived inherent moral depravity of plagiarists (p. 52). Lindey's other major contribution is his articulation that plagiarism cannot be considered a simple ethical binary issue because "divergent views of borrowing [have] done much to confuse appraisals of plagiarism" (p. 232).

Marsh (2004) echoes Lindey's central point that plagiarism is considered dishonorable only when tied to romantic notions of authorship as independent, creative, and original. Marsh extends this point to argue that more contemporary notions of plagiarism reflect "a kind of false claim of ownership, in the specific sense of property transgression" that continues to interfere with the practice of teaching and learning in postsecondary education (p. 43). Teaching and learning are interrupted because faculty, in an effort to control plagiarism and protect notions of intellectual capital, are forced to engage with the students as detectives rather than as teachers, advisors, or mentors. The focus on controlling plagiarism among students is critiqued as unnecessarily legalistic and the rules more rigid than those necessarily accorded to intellectual property law (Marsh, 2004).

Additional critiques of the way in which postsecondary education institutions respond to student plagiarism continue along the lines of the argument established by Lindey and reinforced by Marsh. Specifically, Howard (1995, 2000a, 2000b) and Maruca (2001, 2003, 2005) are two of the most prolific contemporary writers in the societal dimension. These writings provide for the most direct critique of the assumptions of the internal dimension, that is, that students who fail to cite or attribute their sources are either ethically corrupt or ethically ignorant. According to Howard and Maruca, these two major assumptions are highly negative and not constructive for truly understanding and resolving the problem because they ignore societal forces that shape definitions of legitimate academic work. So while the internal dimension positions the use of technology to copy and paste as evidence of immorality, the societal dimension argues that technology challenges standard writing conventions and the moral assumptions of plagiarism.

Technologies such as Napster-type peer-to-peer file-sharing software are changing the way people work together by blurring physical boundaries and facilitating connections between people previously unimagined. These technologies "reinforce, amplify, revise, and extend" (Vaidhyanathan, 2004, p. 20) the challenges to the dominant cultural assumptions of information as personal property and knowledge as independently constructed (Bertram Gallant, 2006). Writings in the societal perspective question and then critique previously uncritiqued assumptions of the inherent goodness, universality, and absoluteness of independence, originality, and authorship (Valentine, 2006).

Authors who write about the societal dimension such as Ede and Lundsford (2001) do not suggest the elimination of notions of individual authorship and the unconditional acceptance of copying and collaboration in its place. Rather, the societal dimension highlights the need to consider both and the importance of deconstructing how the idea of the "individual author" might be serving (or not serving) the goals of teaching (learning), service, and research. For instance, is student learning enhanced when "disparate textual practices" such as patch writing and fraud are treated "under a single heading called plagiarism and academic dishonesty," or does it disempower students (Howard, 2000a, p. 85)? Postsecondary education institutions are urged to step back from the mindless or fear-based ready adoption of the "turnitin culture" (Maruca, 2005) to allow for such question asking in the spirit of enhancing academic integrity and the teaching and learning environment. The next subsection reviews the connections between the multidimensional nature of misconduct and contemporary organizational strategies.

The Four Dimensions and Contemporary Organizational Strategies

For the most part, contemporary organizational strategies to stop students from cheating attend to the internal and organizational dimensions of academic misconduct. As mentioned earlier, both the rule compliance and integrity strategies emerged out of the honor code legacy, which locates the problem and the solution in the individual student and the student body. The rule compliance strategy, however, which relies heavily on a disciplinary approach to resolving a perceived student deviancy problem, tends less to the organizational dimensions of misconduct. The rule compliance strategy may focus on reducing opportunities for rule violations (through disciplinary and structural remedies), while the integrity strategy focuses on enhancing the morality or honor of the individual student and larger student body. One reason for the failures of the rule compliance and integrity strategies may be that they fail to address the classroom climate or institutional and societal dimensions of the issue. Exhibit 3 shows how each strategy might address the four dimensions of academic misconduct.

The danger with both strategies is that the focus on reforming the student actor limits the attention paid to classroom dynamics, institutional features, and societal forces, which all contribute to the shaping of academic misconduct. In ignoring these dimensions, educational institutions may appear to be patronizing, self-aggrandizing, and lacking integrity (Bok, 1990; McBee, 1978; Puka, 2005). So although most postsecondary education institutions express concerns about the teaching and learning environment, students and their parents may not take this rhetoric seriously if student academic integrity continues to be considered in isolation from the academic integrity of other players (that is, faculty and administrators) and from the organizational, institutional, and societal contexts. To enhance the seriousness with which people are expected to treat academic conduct, "we must shorten the distance between what we preach and what we practice" (McBee, 1978, p. 32). If integrity is going to be preached, then the practice needs to move beyond the stopping of students from cheating to addressing academic misconduct by faculty and administrators and enhancing the integrity of institutional and societal systems (Puka, 2005).

Summary

This chapter reviewed the research on academic misconduct from a multidisciplinary perspective and suggested that the issue has four dimensions: internal, organizational, institutional, and societal. Each dimension highlights different levels—from micro to macro—of the academic misconduct problem, all of which are important to understand. Viewed through only one of these dimensions, academic misconduct may be understood too simplistically, and organizational responses may be less robust and effective. The heavy reliance on the rule compliance and integrity strategies in contemporary colleges and universities suggests that the internal, organizational, and, to a lesser

EXHIBIT 3
The Dimensions of Dominant Organizational Strategies

	Rule-Compliance Strategy	Integrity Strategy
Internal	Change the internal drive to cheat by disciplining misconduct harshly and consistently when it occurs	Change the internal drive to cheat by developing students' moral and ethical reasoning
Organizational		
Classroom Dynamics	Ask instructors to clearly state the rules for conduct in their classroom	Ask instructors to talk about academic integrity in their classroom
	Encourage the implementation of structural strategies to reduce opportunities for cheating (for example, spacing students apart in examinations)	Encourage the creation of a classroom ethos of trust and honesty by incorporating conversations of integrity and ethics into the curriculum
Peer Norms	Publish academic misconduct statistics and sanctions levied against students for rule violations	Implement an honor code along with symbolic honor pledges and signing ceremonies
	Remove rule violators from the campus so they cannot negatively affect the peer culture	Involve students in creating a "culture of integrity" through honor councils or other bodies

(continued)

EXHIBIT 3 (*continued*)
The Dimensions of Dominant Organizational Strategies

	Rule-Compliance Strategy	Integrity Strategy
Institutional	Increase the costs of student cheating (for example, XF grade on transcript)	Counter the institutional dimension with messages about the importance of ethical conduct and appeals to personal integrity over external measures of success
	Increase the costs to faculty for not reporting misconduct (for example, creating policies that sanction faculty)	Increase the rewards for developing ethical reasoning (for example, remove the XF after ethical training)
Societal	Counter societal dimension by reinforcing traditional rules through use of new media (for example, employ plagiarism detection software)	Counter societal dimension by articulating a valuing of "your own work in your own words" as implicit in personal integrity and honor

extent, institutional dimensions have been emphasized. Unfortunately, though, neither strategy fully takes into account the ways in which classroom dynamics and institutional and societal forces communicate messages that may counter or complicate the rule compliance and integrity messages. The rule compliance strategy, for instance, increases the costs for academic misconduct by enforcing harsh sanctions but neglects to attend to the institutionally embedded rewards for undetected cheating (for example, higher grades). On the other hand, the societal dimension by itself negates the importance of developing students as ethical citizens who should feel personally accountable for institutional integrity.

Acknowledging the multidimensional nature of academic misconduct opens the discussion of the problem more broadly to consider the problem in the context of postsecondary education in the twenty-first century. The historical review demonstrated that definitions and rates of academic misconduct have grown over time as the types of learning assessments and student populations have expanded. So what might be the organizational, institutional, and societal forces that affect academic integrity in the twenty-first century college or university? And how might those forces modulate the effectiveness of the dominant rule compliance and integrity strategies? These questions are addressed in the next section.

Twenty-First Century Forces Shaping Academic Integrity

FAST-PACED CHANGE AND COMPLEX PROBLEMS can affect organizations (Wagoner, 1968). The "cultural strain" created by changing and complex challenges can stretch "old securities [and] common assumptions" to the point where established institutions either break down or reinvent themselves (p. 19). As new or expanding societal forces challenge the assumptions and securities of the postsecondary education institution around issues of authorship, teaching, and learning, it is plausible that academic misconduct may be a manifestation of resulting cultural strains. This section addresses four forces that seem to particularly challenge common assumptions and reshape notions of academic integrity: technology, academic capitalism, institutional constraints, and diversity. The next section addresses the resulting strains on the teaching and learning environment when these forces are ignored or downplayed by contemporary organizational strategies.

Technology

In much of the literature on academic conduct and in particular on student academic conduct, the proliferation and sophistication of technology is cited as the predominant and almost immutable force acting against institutional integrity. Although the postsecondary education institution is fully integrating technology into structures and processes, it is also to an extent fighting technology's influence on the culture and on the teaching and learning relationship. Thus, technology is often cited as a blight on student conduct or a crutch that students use to complete their academic requirements (Eckstein, 2003). The general perception is that technology, specifically the Internet and the capability to virtually connect to multiple resources simultaneously, makes it easier for students and others to "cheat," whether in the form of buying term papers from Internet sites (such as schoolsucks.com or cheathouse.com) or receiving help on homework assignments (Jesdanun, 2005).

Although certainly the Internet can be used constructively to enhance learning, the concern among postsecondary education campuses in connection with student conduct is that an excessive dependence on the Internet will produce a diminished caliber of professionals who are incapable of independent work. Moreover, with the multitude of resources available through technology, students could, in extreme probabilities, graduate from a university without ever having written their own paper or struggled by themselves through a challenging assignment. Thus, institutions often respond by defining the unauthorized use of these Web sites as academic misconduct. This blanket response, though, neglects the complexity of the issue precipitated by the ways in which technological inventions may be redefining concepts of information, authorship, and knowledge; challenging the expertise of educational institutions; and reshaping the nature of academic work (Batson and Bass, 1996; Bertram Gallant, 2006; Gumport and Chun, 1999; Howard, 1995; Keeling, 2004; Maruca, 2003, 2005; Muelder, 1978; Oblinger and Rush, 1997; Park, 2003; Tapscott, 1998; Vaidhyanathan, 2004).

Redefining Concepts of Information, Authorship, and Knowledge

The impact of technology cannot be ignored because "it shapes what counts as knowledge, how knowledge is produced, how people are involved in the production of knowledge, and how an academic knowledge is valued" (Gumport and Chun, 1999, p. 378). Evidence to support this statement can be found in the workplace as the collaborative worker is quickly replacing the independent worker as the standard. And the resulting conflicts and tensions are made manifest in the university as students transpose that standard into their academic work. The "unauthorized collaboration" case at Duke University involving dozens of first year MBA students is just one publicized example (Young, 2007). The complexity of academic integrity arises because there is no "unified front" regarding conceptions of knowledge, information, and academic work (Howard, 1995, p. 793).

Technological challenges to dominant academic conceptions are not recent phenomena. The printing press has been credited with creating the notion of the independent author (Howard, 1995; Vaidhyanathan, 2001). The transformation of writing into a commercial enterprise eventually led to the establishment of copyrights laws to "protect" the intellectual works of independent authors and encourage efforts at creative productions (Vaidhyanathan, 2001). The evolving belief was that if ideas and words could be "stolen," authors could not profit from their works and they would stop writing. Thus, the invention of the printing press and the resulting commercialization of literary works created the need to root out and punish plagiarists who "fail to conform to at least two sets of laws: those pertaining to traditional ideas of authorship and those more recent inventions designed to protect the rights and privileges of authors" (Marsh, 2004, p. 23). In other words, a technological invention both helped to define a specific type of academic misconduct (that is, plagiarism) as well as to increase the ease of engaging in that very behavior. The monetary value of written works is instilled in each subsequent generation by enforcing rules of citation and attribution and punishing those who break those rules.

The calculator is another technological invention that has redefined ideas of knowledge in the academy. When the calculator entered the academic classroom, the typical institutional response was outrage over the ways in which it could facilitate students' "cheating" (Gamerman, 2006). After time, however, critics began to argue that the calculator was simply challenging formula memorization and mental calculations as the ultimate goals of education. Critics saw optimism in the calculator's potential to "transform the learner from calculator to critical thinker," to free up students to use "brain power to think critically, to communicate clearly, to solve mathematical problems, and to apply mathematics to complex scientific and social problems" (Lacampagne, 1993, p. 9).

Beyond the printing press and the calculator, the computer is perhaps the most invasive technological invention in that it profoundly affects all areas of academic work, whether in math or English classes or in independent or collaborative assignments. The twenty-first-century traditional-age college student was raised in the era of the computer and, as such, may view information, learning, and knowledge differently from previous generations (Bruster, 2004; Tapscott, 1998). Take, for example, plagiarism and unauthorized collaboration, the behaviors in which students most readily engage yet consider as two of the least serious forms of cheating (Brimble and Stevenson-Clarke, 2006; Brown and Howell, 2001; Franklyn-Stokes and Newstead, 1995; Levy and Rakovski, 2006; McCabe, 2005b; McCabe and Trevino, 1996; Zelna and Bresciani, 2004). Over a thirty-year period, the number of students who self-report engaging in unauthorized collaboration has tripled (McCabe and Bowers, 1994), and more recent studies have found that students and faculty rate copying from the Internet without attribution as a less serious form of academic misconduct (Levy and Rakovski, 2006; Robinson-Zañartu and others, 2005). These studies suggest that technology has precipitated disparate and complicated conceptions of legitimate or ethical academic practices (Townley and Parsell, 2004; Wilson, 2004).

Vaidhyanathan (2004) argues that changing conceptions of knowledge, information, and legitimate academic work are a result of "peer-to-peer technology" that offers "a fuller realization of knowledge and power for the common good" because millions of people take from the storehouse of knowledge (p. 21). Thus, information-sharing technology is creating a sense of a "collective intelligence" and a "hacker ethic [that] rest on openness, peer review, individual economy, and communal responsibility" (Vaidhyanathan, 2004, p. 39). This hacker ethic may conflict with the institutional ethic of individual effort and independent work, and when it does, institutions tend to categorize the first as academic misconduct and the latter as academic integrity.

Challenging the Expertise of Educational Institutions

In my role as academic integrity coordinator, I once received a report of academic misconduct from an instructor who claimed that a student violated the integrity policy by using the Internet to develop ideas for her assignment. The instructor had told the students that they could speak with their peers about the assignment and brainstorm together ways in which to approach the topic, but he saw the use of the Internet as a violation of his policy. Not only may it be difficult for students to understand such a nuanced distinction made as that between consulting with in-class peers versus consulting with "virtual peers," but even if students could understand this distinction and not view it as artificial or unnecessary, the distinction itself may inadvertently penalize students who do not possess cultural capital in that particular class, subject area, or institution.

The Internet, in other words, has democratized access to expertise that previously was in the control of the privileged few (Connell, 1981). It is significantly easier in the twenty-first century for students to find an abundance of information on any topic and to gather expert opinions and ideas, whether they are attending Harvard or the local community college. A simple Internet search on "homework help from experts" retrieves thousands of hits, from free public library services to for-profit companies around the world that offer resources and help to students of all ages (see homeworkelephant.co.uk, cramster.com, or gethomeworkhelp.com). As a result of this information explosion, colleges and universities that continue to function as if they are the primary purveyors, repositories, or distributors of information and knowledge may be on the losing end (Duderstadt, Atkins, and Van Houweling, 2002). With the possibilities of the Internet, students may no longer see the necessity of attending traditional universities, visiting university libraries, or attending classes to access expert knowledge or information.

Reshaping the Nature of Academic Work

Although the "banking" model of education (that is, knowledge is considered something that can be deposited in students) has survived previous challenges (Barr and Tagg, 1994; Bruffee, 1984; Magolda, 1999; Palmer, 1998), it is now under a more pronounced threat by technological advances. The "napsterization of knowledge" challenges norms for academic conduct such as the preference for independent versus collaborative work (Boynton, 2001). The premise of Internet sites such as Wikipedia and technology such as sharepoint (see sharepoint.com) is that work, ideas, knowledge, and information will be shared among multiple parties. Such conflicting notions of information (personal versus communal property) and knowledge (independently versus collaboratively constructed) hint that academic integrity is less an individual character trait than it is a social phenomenon located at the nexus of teaching and learning (Bertram Gallant, 2006).

If academic integrity is a social phenomenon, then several questions are intimated. Will students believe it is unethical to collaborate on homework assignments or problems if knowledge is thought to be collaboratively constructed? If information is thought of as communal property, will students understand (or agree with) the requirements for citation and attribution? Some studies have shown that students may in fact not understand these requirements (Evans and Craig, 1990; Franklyn-Stokes and Newstead, 1995). Today's college students are used to employing technology as a way to control their educational experiences—they are working together, forming their own study groups, and seeking out answers to their questions, that is, they are being active learners (Duderstadt, Atkins, and Van Houweling, 2002). In a sense, "electronic technologies have made the process of learning and teaching more visible and public" (Hutchings, 2002, p. 13) and subsequently illuminated the institutional constraints that strain the teaching and learning environment.

Institutional Constraints

Individuals do not operate in a vacuum but in institutions that themselves are complex and replete with competing interests and priorities. In understanding academic integrity in the twenty-first century, it is important to understand how institutional constraints may inhibit the effectiveness of predominant organizational strategies. The reconciliation of professorial, student, or administrator misconduct using rule compliance and integrity strategies is doubtful without the redress of these institutional constraints (Schurr, 1982). This notion of "institutional constraints" comes from Arnstine (1978). Arnstine suggested that teaching development centers would have limited effectiveness in actually improving teaching because they do not address the institutional features that constrain good teaching such as large classrooms, an emphasis on research, educational commercialization, and various systems such as reading, scheduling, and tenure and promotion.

Contemporary literature on academic integrity suggests that some "constraints" affect policy compliance on the part of faculty:

A perceived or real lack of institutional or administrative support for enforcement;

An unwillingness to take the role of cop or "ogre" and engage in confrontation over the misconduct;

Overburdened by committee, teaching, and publishing responsibilities;

Teaching in large classes, which makes academic misconduct difficult to monitor;

Rewards for conducting research and publishing and penalties (in costs of time and energy) for reporting or monitoring misconduct; and

A fear of consequences such as retribution or harassment by the charged student or damage of the student's academic or career future (Alschuler and Blimling, 1995; Bertram Gallant, 2007; Decoo, 2002; Hutton, 2006; Jendrek, 1989; Laney, 1990; Larkham and Manns, 2002; McCabe, 1993; Rich, 1984; Rudolph and Timm, 1998; Whitley and Keith-Spiegel, 2001).

Overall, the efforts to police misconduct, follow institutional policies, and prove academic misconduct in evidentiary hearings place additional burdens on faculty that are not only unacknowledged and rewarded but also emotionally draining. Often, educational institutions do not take into account that the "time required to produce evidence" is burdensome for the "pressured academic" and that participating in judicial hearings causes "very real stress" with few benefits (Larkham and Manns, 2002, p. 347). It is often why faculty favor the integrity strategy, which promises that faculty workload will be reduced because students will stop each other from cheating.

Institutional constraints inhibit students' desire or ability to comply with codes of conduct:

A teaching or evaluation oriented rather than a learning oriented environment;

Lack of venues for disagreeing with those in power on acceptable means for completing academic work;

Perceptions of normative behavior (cheating) that counter institutionally desired norms (academic integrity);

Lack of information on the policy and nature of academic misconduct;

Loyalty to peers, which often conflicts with loyalty to community and constrains students from abiding by institutional policies; and

Competing interests such as employment and extracurricular activities (Drinan, 1999; Christensen Hughes and McCabe, 2006; Jordan, 2001; Larkham and Manns, 2002; McCabe and Trevino, 2002; Stearns, 2001; Whitley and Keith-Spiegel, 2001).

Institutional constraints do not make unethical behavior acceptable, but they do create ethical dilemmas for the actors. Although integrity policies or honor codes may make explicit preferred behavioral expectations, institutional structures and norms may imply other, contradictory expectations (Smith and Reynolds, 1990). Students and faculty must then choose whether to follow the explicit or the implicit expectations because there is "no simple moral equation" indicating how instructors and students should balance their various obligations (Callahan, 1982, p. 339). For example, expectations for tenure and promotion such as publishing and positive teaching evaluations may conflict with an expectation that faculty report all academic misconduct cases. Laney (1990) further argues this concern: "We can largely count on ethical behavior as long as the overall context for our work is clear, as long as institutional structures shield individuals from unnecessary and unacceptable conflicts of interest. But while we all intend to act honorably, it is foolish to allow people to be placed in situations where they are unduly tested, and where institutional pressures compound the social and personal pressures that weigh on us all" (p. 58).

The persistence of institutional constraints inhibiting the realization of academic integrity may in part be tied to the commercialization of postsecondary education.

Academic Capitalism

Among the many causes of the growth in academic fraud is the fact that participation in formal education beyond the minimum required levels is increasing and that competition to gain credentials for educational, occupational, and social advancement has grown (Eckstein, 2003, p. 17).

Eckstein and others have suggested that commercial interests, grade achievements, research dollars, and enrollments are increasingly receiving greater attention by faculty and institutions and that this attention shift subsequently affects other educational interests such as learning and the development of community (Astin, 1993; Bok, 2003; Eckstein, 2003; Slaughter and Leslie, 1997). In line with these commercial interests and influenced by "time constraints, financial problems, government regulations, and other social pressures" (Besvinick, 1983, p. 569), institutions of postsecondary education may be creating environments that are not as tied to learning imperatives as to more capitalist imperatives (Counelis, 1993). And, Bok (2003) argues, it sets a poor example for students who will be unlikely to adhere to espoused principles of academic integrity if "they perceive that the institution . . . compromises its own moral principles in order to win at football, sign a lucrative research contract, or earn a profit from Internet courses. In deciding how to lead their lives, undergraduates often learn more from the example of those in positions of authority than they do from lectures in the classroom" (p. 109).

In my own research, I found that market or commercial interests are not just subscribed to by students but are reproduced in postsecondary education institutional structures and cultures that "symbolize the academic degree as a product to be consumed rather than an educative experience" (Bertram Gallant, 2006, p. 160). Specifically, the secondary educational system reinforces and emphasizes the acquisition of credits and the bypassing of education requirements to jump-start college. Institutionalized structures such as concurrent enrollment and advanced placement classes reinforce a focus on accumulating credits and enhancing grade point averages (Blizek, 2000; Bok, 2003; David and Kovach, 1979). Thus, students see their bending of other social conventions to accumulate credits and enhance their grade point average as normal rather than morally wrong. It is especially true if parents and high school teachers have been reticent in prohibiting such behaviors (such as the submission of the same paper for credit in two different classes) in the spirit of student educational progress.

The demands of the public and "consumers" of education for outcomes and deliverable products in exchange for their monetary investment may be straining the integrity of the teaching and learning environment (Lederman and Redden, 2007). Faculty and students are increasingly being viewed less as teachers and learners and more as producers of knowledge or as the means for advancing the institution in rankings and prestige (Slaughter and Rhoades, 2004). Thus it should not be a surprise if students and faculty act in ways that undermine the teaching and learning imperative. Yet educational institutions respond not with changes in practice but with demands of individual integrity. David and Kovach (1979) argued the danger of this mixed message almost thirty years ago: "One possible unforeseen consequence of this new emphasis in marketing and commercialization of college and university courses seems to be an increase in student cheating and the emergence of business enterprises [that] are supported by, and help to maintain, this cheating. . . . [This new emphasis, then, may be] undermining . . . the basic goals and values which the university hopes to promote" (p. 343). It could be argued, then, that the capitalist educational system and society are modeling the very behaviors they purport to condemn and that the "morally corrupt" values of students are embedded in the "intellectual and social ethos in which education takes place" (Churchill, 1982, p. 302). Academic capitalism does not create a situation in which academic misconduct is acceptable, but it does complicate notions of academic integrity and cheating.

Diversity

Perhaps one of the more recognized forces complicating notions of academic integrity and academic misconduct on postsecondary education campuses is the diversification of the student population. The monograph earlier noted the correlation between campus diversification and intensifying concern with student cheating during the 1960s and 1970s. The move from a secluded "ivory tower" in which the student population was small and relatively homogeneous to the mass educational system in which the student population is vast and diverse may have strained cultural expectations. For example, it may have been expected (and accepted) that fraternity brothers would share papers and help one another, but when this practice expanded beyond this well-contained situation, cheating became a more serious concern in postsecondary education institutions. And with an expanding and diversified student population, it became substantially more difficult to discern what should be taught, how it should be taught, and how it can best be assessed as a result of the more diverse conceptions of academic work and educational purpose (Shils, 1983).

Institutional diversity in terms of cultures (that is, norms and values), purposes, goals, and missions makes the issue of academic integrity more complex because understandings of legitimate academic conduct are less likely to be shared. Studies have found that not only do American faculty and students have differing conceptions of honest academic work among and between themselves but also that students and faculty from different countries may have differing conceptions from those predominantly held in America (Barnett and Dalton, 1981; Bowden, 1996; Eisenberg, 2004; Howard, 1995; Introna, Hayes, Blair, and Wood, 2003; Kuehn, Stanwyck, and Holland, 1990; McLeod, 1992; Park, 2003; Stanwyck and Abdelal, 1984).

As an example, it has been argued that students raised outside the western Anglo-Saxon culture may not share or understand the values underlying the rules of citation and attribution dominant in American postsecondary education institutions (Bowden, 1996; Leask, 2006; Lin and Wen, 2006; McLeod, 1992; Sowden, 2004; Tucker, 2003). Researchers have found, for instance, that students from cultures in which communal ownership is valued over independent ownership may find it countercultural to cite an idea or phrase as if someone owned it (Lin and Wen, 2006; McLeod, 1992; Sowden, 2004; Tucker, 2003). These differences present ethical dilemmas for students because their choice to comply with the instructor's rules so as not to "cheat" may conflict with other choices that could help them learn, lend aid to a friend, or honor the communal nature of knowledge. Thus, a student's resolution of such an ethical dilemma may not reflect an intent to deceive or a morally corrupt choice even if his or her behavior conflicts with the instructor's expectations (McFall, 1987; Turiel, 1983). Institutional sanctioning or appeals to student morality or integrity to stop students from "cheating," then, may not be effective.

The rule compliance and integrity strategies may also not be effective because they are modeled on the legacy of the honor code, which originated in relatively homogeneous educational institutions—definitely all male and all white and with little variation in socioeconomic status. With such a homogeneous body, it could be expected that to a large extent students might hold the same values or conceptions of the goals and purposes of academic work and the college degree. In fact, Woodrow Wilson himself, as president of Princeton in 1905, argued that a feeling of community and shared understanding among the student body is "a condition precedent to the success of the honor system" and notes that the Princeton student body of 1892–93 had "been conscious of an organic solidarity, unity, singleness in life if not in study, which has made it, not merely a body of individuals, but a real community" (Wilson, 1905, par. 4). Angell (1928) made the same argument: "The value of intimate groups in fostering morale in relation to conduct is well illustrated by the 'honor system' in examinations. This system has had its chief success in relatively small, well established and, with regard to their student bodies, homogeneous colleges or universities. . . . The reason for this appears to be simply that the moral sentiment is then stronger because the individual is more likely to identify himself with the smaller group and because a person hesitates to risk lowering himself in the eyes of those with whom he is on friendly terms" (p. 220).

This positive effect of the honor code seems less probable in a contemporary, diverse institution. McCabe, Trevino, and Butterfield (1999) found that "a significant number of students believe that honor codes make cheating relatively easy" (p. 227) because, rather than tying students to a universal principle, honor codes suggest to the students that everything is permissible. The negative consequence of honor codes may be more pronounced in large universities or classes where community is difficult to develop. Thus, traditional approaches to student academic conduct may not be effective in the diverse institutions of today, which hold multiple and conflicting ideas of acceptable classroom conduct and legitimate academic work. To borrow an idea from Hutchings (2002), who was referring to the scholarship of teaching and learning, the traditional ways of looking at student academic misconduct may be "based on an out-of-date pedagogical model. Perhaps what is needed is a way of framing ethical issues . . . that is better matched to emerging ideas about the classroom and classroom practice" (p. 13).

Summary

The forces and their impacts described in this section suggest that academic misconduct should be examined less as the disease and more as the symptom of a disease: "increases in class sizes, casualisation of tertiary teaching, and the reduction of universities to economic producers undermine the intellectual community in ways that should concern both teachers and students far more than students' misuse of net-trawled material. Internet plagiarism is symptomatic of declining trust and the degrading of the conditions needed to maintain a community strong in intellectual virtue. It is not the disease itself" (Townley and Parsell, 2004, p. 277).

Despite lingering and changing disease symptoms, organizational responses to student academic misconduct in the twenty-first century have not changed substantially from those taken in previous decades. The legacy of the honor code lives on in the rule compliance and integrity strategies. The same structural solutions to student cheating implemented in the early twentieth century (for example, spacing students apart in examinations, checking identification when students hand in assignments) continue today, most likely with greater frequency, given the expansion of postsecondary education over the last one hundred years. These symbolic, structural, and procedural interventions are all implemented with the intent to stop students from cheating. Yet the perception exists that academic misconduct continues to thrive and spread, creating a cheating culture.

It is possible that the age-old methods, while practical, may not be particularly effective in the context of the complex twenty-first century institution. Unaddressed institutional constraints continue to interfere with faculty and student rule compliance. Academic capitalism suggests to students and faculty that integrity may not matter if the end result is a viable, useful product that will benefit the college or university. Moreover, the tendency to view student academic misconduct as another form of students behaving badly (along with, for example, binge drinking) ignores changing conceptions of information, knowledge, and pedagogy caused by technology and the diversification of postsecondary education campuses. That is, a focus on stopping students from "cheating" without considering the complexity of academic integrity could be in the end "counterproductive" to the teaching and learning imperative (Eble, 1977, p. 122). The next section further explores the counterproductive strains on the teaching and learning environment.

Strains on the Teaching and Learning Environment

CAMPUSES DO NOT NORMALLY ENGAGE in an academic integrity initiative simply to reduce academic misconduct by students but to reach multiple related goals. One goal of the rule compliance and integrity strategies is to improve the faculty-student relationship, which may otherwise be harmed by cheating and dishonesty. Developing student integrity is thought to reduce the work faculty have to do to control cheating in their classrooms, and both strategies aim to ensure a fair assessment of student learning. The promise of the integrity strategy is that students will develop as ethical citizens, both in the academy and beyond. With the focus on student conduct, however, the rule compliance and integrity strategies neglect the multiple dimensions of the issue and the strains caused by the forces affecting the teaching and learning environment of the twenty-first century. As a result, the laudable goals of the dominant organizational strategies may not be realized. This section describes the strains on the teaching and learning environment that may limit the effectiveness of the dominant organizational strategies.

On the Faculty-Student Relationship

"One of the dimensions for me of the problem of plagiarism . . . is the comic peculiarity of my claiming to be committed to helping students learn but sometimes spending large chunks of everyone's time trying to corner them in a fraud. Then there is the distance, the surprising separation I discover in such situations between myself and students. Because I assume their good will and candor and my own, both their cheating and my response to it shock me. I take for granted that we are working together and thus am amazed each time at the unimagined distance between us" [Murphy, 1990, p. 902].

Murphy's comments represent one of the main strains caused by primarily framing academic integrity along the internal dimension and ignoring the organizational, institutional, and societal forces shaping the issue. In recounting his experience as an instructor, Murphy found himself so immersed in the catching of "thieves" and "liars" that he was unable to join with the student in her learning through the process of writing. Instead, he falsely accused her of plagiarism. A teacher's preoccupation with stopping students from cheating may dichotomize students and their actions as dishonest or honest rather than as struggling or succeeding in learning, which will undoubtedly affect the faculty-student relationship.

Bowden (1996) argued that these negative effects extend beyond the faculty-student relationship to the student's relationship with all potential learning guides: "teacher, tutor, and student fears of transgressing a particular code of ethics actually prevent them from working together effectively on writing and error correction, both mechanical and global" (p. 83). These "fears of transgressing a particular code of ethics" further divide teachers and students along lines of power and authority rather than enjoining them as partners in learning. Kilpatrick, an educational theorist, argued:

> *We have seen the evil tendency toward cramming. In its extreme form this may be found as cheating. Perhaps most of all is it true that education, to be morally educative, requires that children live as a social group in the school with the teacher as the comrade and social arbiter. But if assignment and penalty be stressed, an opposition between teacher and pupil is all but inevitable. This means that the child spends from eight to twelve years of his life thinking of those in closest authority over him as his opponents. A good part of his efforts will be spent in "beating the game" [cited in Chipman and McDonald, 1982, p. 464].*

The "opposition between teacher and pupil" may be an inevitable part of the educational system that is built on assessments and evaluations, but the game of stopping students from cheating may reinforce this opposition rather than attempt to disquiet it (Bruffee, 1984; Eble, 1977; Introna, Hayes, Blair, and Wood, 2003). Howard (2001) argues this point: "In our stampede to fight what *The New York Times* calls a 'plague' of plagiarism, we risk becoming the enemies rather than the mentors of our students; we are replacing the student-teacher relationship with the criminal-police relationship" (p. B24).

On the Role of Faculty

With a change in the faculty-student relationship comes a strain on the way faculty perform their role as teacher. The criminal-police relationship emphasized in the attempt to stop students from cheating reifies the authoritative role of the faculty member in the classroom. This emphasis not only affects the learning process and the role of students but also strains the role of faculty as mentor, guide, and facilitator. Faculty become so focused on stopping students from cheating that they spend more time designing assessments in ways to reduce cheating rather than enhance learning.

Proponents of the integrity strategy use this observation as an argument against the rule compliance strategy; if the responsibility for ensuring students' honor and integrity is placed in the hands of the students, faculty are released from their role as police officers. This view neglects the forces that shape new ideas of information, knowledge, and academic integrity among the student population, however; if students do not consider an act as cheating, they will be unlikely to monitor that behavior on behalf of faculty. Thus, even on campuses that employ the integrity strategy, faculty are left to operate as police officers to monitor behaviors about which the parties disagree; in my experience, faculty are most often put into this role when collaboration or the use of aids (such as old exams, lab reports, or papers) is the activity in question.

On the Learning Process

A moral panic about students' actions such as unauthorized collaboration, use of unauthorized resources, and cutting and pasting written works may inadvertently interfere with practices that otherwise afford students excellent learning opportunities. For example, a common practice of academic misconduct among students is copying and pasting material from the Internet into their assigned papers. This practice can be framed as problematic in at least two ways.

The first and more popular is to frame the act as plagiarism or "cheating" and the student a "plagiarist." This framing focuses on telling the student that what she did was ethically wrong and a violation of institutional policies for which she will be sanctioned. The logic is, of course, that the punishment will teach the student not to copy and paste. Unfortunately, this framing does not necessarily help the student *learn* how not to copy and paste (that is, learn how to be a writer). Townley and Parsell (2004) argue this point: "to look for a solution from turnitin, for example, is to treat our students as resources, to allow their knowledge and truth-seeking to be commodified. It is hard to imagine that such an approach will encourage our students to engage with us and the broader academic community in a trustworthy manner. If we treat our students as resources or instruments, how can we expect them to see the academy as anything more than a resource for them to exploit?" (p. 276).

An alternative response is to frame the act as symbolic of a student writer's lack of skill and the development she still requires to become a writer who can produce interesting pieces of work that do not depend on the work of others. The appropriate organizational response in this case would be to grade the student based on her level of writing and comprehension and then work with her to improve her skills and confidence as an independently capable writer. If the concern is that she tried to "cheat the system" by using others' words to earn a higher grade, the first response is appropriate. Alternatively, if the concern is that she has not yet learned to write in a way that builds on others' ideas rather than just copy them, then the second response is more appropriate.

When educational institutions become so focused on catching cheaters, then, the learning that is valued in the process may actually be lost. This risk may be particularly acute in the case of collaboration because institutions have not necessarily been successful at both encouraging and disciplining collaboration in the spirit of enhancing learning (Drinan, 1999). Unfortunately, the potential of loss is great because research has shown that students learn more when they are thinking, applying, collaborating, and problem solving than when they are memorizing or working independently (Kuh and others, 2005). Vaidhyanathan (2001) argued a parallel process in the overreach of copyright laws, which can in fact limit the very creativity they attempt to protect. Similarly, Goodstein (1991) argued that the rules and regulations implemented to control scientific fraud can hinder the discovery of new ideas and concepts, thus hindering "scientific progress" (p. 509).

On Evolving Ideas of Teaching and Learning

Learning is different in the digital age from what it was fifty or one hundred years ago, yet institutions and pedagogies have not significantly changed (Duderstadt, Atkins, and Van Houweling, 2002). Some authors have thus suggested that academic misconduct may be less about the failures of students and more about the failures of instructors and institutions to rethink teaching and learning in this "new electronic environment" (Townley and Parsell, 2004, p. 276). This failure to rethink teaching and learning could in part be an outcome of the excessive concern with protecting the grading and evaluation systems from student corruption.

Take, for example, the use of a cell phone to obtain answers while writing an exam. Most would consider this practice a blatant act of academic misconduct in a system that depends on the use of examinations to test a student's independent knowledge and abilities. And in such an educational system, the act should be considered misconduct and treated accordingly because it is not fair to those students who completed the exam independently without cheating. At the same time, this practice raises some interesting considerations beyond stopping the student from cheating. For instance, how is technology, with its capabilities to connect people and resources, slowly changing what and how students should be learning? Will students need to attend college or university in the future to receive knowledge from experts or be tested on the ability to apply what one has memorized? How is technology changing the forms of evaluations that should be used?

These questions are just some of the intriguing ones that emerge when considering academic integrity as a teaching and learning imperative. Thus, as campuses continue to work to enhance academic integrity, it may be time to also reconsider methods for teaching and assessment that work with rather than fight against the digital world of the future.

On the Development of Students

Faculty hold differing conceptions of academic integrity, and they have the academic freedom to define expectations for it in their individual classes (Brimble and Stevenson-Clarke, 2006; Robinson-Zañartu and others, 2005; Roig, 2001; Seriup Pincus and Pedhazur Schmelkin, 2003). As a result, codes of conduct necessarily have to distill broad statements of integrity and honor down to a basic rule—what is authorized by the professor is academic integrity and what is not authorized is academic misconduct. Unfortunately, this distillation requires clear communication of expectations by all faculty in all classes so that students know for each assignment what behaviors are authorized and what are not; in the grayness over the definitions of academic misconduct looms a "bigger burden on teachers to make the rules crystal clear" (Gamerman, 2006, P1). For example, are students allowed to use test or essay banks located on campus? What about those off campus or online? When are students allowed to collaborate and when are they not, and how do they draw the ambiguous line between independent and collaboratively constructed knowledge?

The distillation of the ambiguity of academic integrity into specific rules not only overly burdens faculty but may also inhibit the development of students. Students who are trained to work only in authorized ways may be disempowered as self-authorized learners, defined as people who can actively participate in their own learning (Kegan, 1994; Magolda, 1999). Students in such environments who equate ethics and integrity to obedience to rules may also not develop as ethically responsible learners who can see multiple possibilities, organize complex experiences, make sense of them, and make decisions (Armentrout, 1979; Bruffee, 1984; Starratt, 1994).

The negative effects of this distillation may be particularly palatable in the debate over independent versus collaborative learning. For example, in the mathematics department on my campus, the notion of "unauthorized collaboration" is foreign because student collaboration is seen as a valuable way to learn. Thus, collaboration is always implicitly authorized in the math department. But students intellectually empowered in such an environment may find themselves lost and confused in their general education or humanities classes, where independent and original thought are considered not only superior but also more moral. Students who, empowered by the potential of collaboration for enhancing their learning (and their grades), employ that method of work in classes requiring independent writing may be charged with misconduct and told that they are intellectually dishonest or, perhaps worse, cheaters. After some time, students may refrain from self-authorizing as active learners for fear of crossing that elusive line between collaboration and cheating.

Another practical example from my own experience may be particularly illustrative at this time. As part of my work responsibilities, I present information about the university's integrity policy and definitions of academic misconduct to teaching assistants. After the presentation, one of the attendees came to me, visibly upset and somewhat flustered and confused. During the course of my presentation, this student came to the conclusion that she had in fact been dishonest throughout her academic career, including her current one as a Ph.D. student in engineering. She conveyed to me the following story:

"When I'm assigned problems to work through, I use the book assigned by the professor. However, if at the end of that exercise, I still feel like I need more practice in order to truly learn and understand the concepts, I go to the library to find another textbook on the same subject, and I work through those problems and check my answers against the solutions to determine if I am mastering the subject. Now I am concerned that I have been cheating."

When I assured her that her actions simply indicated that she was being a good student, she replied, "But the instructor did not authorize that I could use those as aids in helping me learn, so it must be cheating." I had to admit that the instructor could charge her with a violation of the policy if he determined her behavior to be intellectually dishonest. Ultimately, I believe that a hearing panel would find her not responsible for academic misconduct in such a case, but I also suspect that the experience would negatively impact her as a self-authorized learner and influence her not to take responsibility for her own learning. The problem with disempowering students in this way is that "conformity, not critical thinking, is the product of such academic enterprises" (Young, 1997, p. 133).

Summary

Technology, institutional constraints, academic capitalism, and diversity are forces in the twenty-first century postsecondary education institution that interact with the predominance of the rule compliance and integrity strategies in ways that strain the teaching and learning environment and call for pedagogical reform (Hart and Graham, n.d.). The relationship between the student and the teacher or tutor, the role of faculty, the evolution of teaching and learning, and the development of learners can all be negatively affected by a focus on stopping students from cheating. Clear rules and guidelines are necessary so that students know what conduct is acceptable in certain contexts, but a preoccupation with stopping students from cheating may result in the legislation of the teaching and learning process.

When changing conceptions of knowledge, information, learning, and the purpose of postsecondary education are responded to with a tightening and proliferation of rules, every interaction between student and teacher becomes legislated. The legislation of teaching and learning invites legal interference with the work of faculty and students in the classroom, especially as postsecondary education continues to become absolutely essential to people's financial well-being. Neither the consumers of postsecondary education (that is, the students and parents) nor the courts will find favor with institutions that place the entire burden for academic integrity on the shoulders of students. According to Smith and Reynolds (1990):

> *Most difficult decisions involve problems of balancing legitimate competing claims, not simple choices between doing right and doing wrong. They arise out of the multiple agendas and demands made upon an institution. . . . The problem of responsible decision-making amid competing claims is further complicated by the number of significant values tensions that appear to be inherent in the academic enterprise. . . . These tensions . . . cannot be eliminated; the challenge is to see creative possibilities in the tension [p. 23].*

The next section explores one creative possibility to enhance academic integrity as an intimate part of the teaching and learning imperative.

A New Approach to Academic Integrity: The Teaching and Learning Strategy

PREVIOUS SECTIONS I HAVE ILLUSTRATED the complex history and contemporary state of student academic misconduct as well as the strains caused by organizational strategies that ignore forces shaping education in the twenty-first century. This section calls for a new organizational strategy for addressing academic misconduct, one that transfers the focus from student conduct and character to teaching and learning. The teaching and learning strategy does not negate the import of establishing and enforcing conduct standards or developing students as ethical and responsible citizens but instead encompasses those disciplinary and developmental methods into a more robust and comprehensive approach. This new strategy expands the repertoire to include pedagogical methods and expands the audience from students to faculty in particular but also to staff and administrators. The essence of this strategy is the reframing of the main practical question from "how do we stop students from cheating?" to "how do we ensure students are learning?"

Asking how to ensure that students are learning shifts the focus of the discussion from the micro to the macrolevel. This shift in focus enables campuses to consider the multidimensional nature of the issue and to address the internal, organizational, institutional, and societal dimensions of the problem. It is unknown whether any campuses currently adopt a teaching and learning strategy in response to the problem of academic misconduct, so the elements of this strategy are derived from academic integrity, assessment, teaching and learning literature, and practical experiences. Research is needed to ascertain the prevalence and effectiveness of each of the three strategies described in this monograph.

Defining the Teaching and Learning Strategy

The teaching and learning strategy for enhancing integrity in academic work originates out of more broad-based strategies to improve learning in postsecondary education settings (Association of American Colleges and Universities; 2002; Astin, 1996; Barr and Tagg, 1994; Donald, 1997; Guskin, 1994). The strategy primarily suggests that the integrity of students' academic work is intimately linked to the learning environment, which includes "the campus and the social milieu, the disciplines that provide the knowledge environment, the students in the arrangements made for them, the teaching and learning process, and the assessment of learning, instruction, and programs" (Donald, 1997, p. xii). Thus, the strategy attends not just to the rule compliance or integrity of the individual student or student population but to the integrity of the institutional environment as a whole.

The suggestion for a learning focus is not unlike those made by integrity strategists such as Whitley and Keith-Spiegel (2002), McCabe and Drinan (1999), and McCabe and Pavela (n.d.), who argue that a learning-oriented environment, awareness of external forces affecting academic integrity, enhanced student-faculty contact, and better teaching can all enhance students' academic integrity. Unlike in the integrity strategy, however, the teaching and learning process and environment are forefront in the teaching and learning strategy. Without a clear focus by institutional leaders, administrators, and faculty on the learning environment, organizational responses to students' academic misconduct will necessarily be distilled down to the internal dimension.

Smith and Reynolds (1990) caution that enhancing the integrity of the academic enterprise "demands that we move beyond concerns with wrongdoing and isolated issues" (p. 29) to an understanding of systemic issues that are altering the postsecondary education landscape. Thus, rather than simply perceiving students' academic misconduct as a problem to resolve, the behaviors and the varying perceptions should be seized "to open up discussions of the institution's essential values and bring to these occasions a strong sense of which values [postsecondary education leaders] believe must be preserved or nurtured" (Smith and Reynolds, 1990, p. 29). The teaching and learning strategy redirects campuses from attaching an overpowering importance to the machinery of catching and reforming student cheaters to the pedagogy, curriculum, methods, and institutional structures that will facilitate learning. In this way academic integrity can be reconsidered not as a solution to students' cheating but as an issue of teaching and learning that involves all organizational members.

It is suggested here that the teaching and learning strategy has four main goals: fostering a learning-oriented environment, improving instruction, enhancing institutional support for teaching and learning, and reducing institutional constraints to teaching and learning integrity.

Fostering a Learning-Oriented Environment

Researchers have found that students who admit to cheating perceive their classroom environment to be "less personalized, less involving, less cohesive, less satisfying, less task oriented, and less individualized" (Pulvers and Diekhoff, 1999, p. 495). Thus, rather than convincing students to stop cheating, the goal of the teaching and learning strategy is to foster a learning-oriented environment that will motivate students to engage in the course material. A learning-oriented environment could be developed by instituting "small class sizes, curricular and extracurricular activities focusing on the personal and intellectual development of their students, and an atmosphere of collegiality and mutual respect among students, faculty members, administrators, and staff members" (Whitley and Keith-Spiegel, 2002, p. 150). Though admittedly difficult in the competitive, grade-oriented postsecondary education environment of the twenty-first century, it is not an unreasonable goal (Donald, 1997). A learning-oriented environment would highlight and measure success in terms of "student learning and intellectual development" rather than by products and revenue generation (Whitley and Keith-Spiegel, 2002, p. 150). How might it be done?

Faculty can create a learning-oriented environment by focusing on pedagogical strategies and assessment methods that "involve choice, challenge, control, and collaboration," which have been shown to "improve students' attitudes toward learning" (Donald, 1997, p. 101). This solution is both particularly difficult and extremely important in larger classes where students experience a greater sense of isolation and anonymity, both of which can contribute to academic misconduct (Pulvers and Diekhoff, 1999). Another common feature of larger introductory classes that may undermine learning and contribute to students' academic misconduct is the instructor who "sets the same essays, issues the same case studies, or asks for reports on tried and tested principles, year after year" (Carroll and Appleton, 2001, p. 9).

Academic misconduct may be tied to the "overpowering importance attached to locating and transferring facts and opinions and the lack of significance given to thinking and independent expression. The answer is not to move the machinery of formal scholarship down into elementary grades, but to diminish greatly the witless gathering and disguising of facts" (Eble, 1977, p. 125). Although faculty are required to test basic disciplinary facts in some classes, a learning-oriented environment can be created by also requiring higher-level tasks, explicating the learning outcomes for each assignment, and modeling the inquiry process (Donald, 1997; Guskin, 1994). Overall, the fostering of a learning-oriented environment must consider the impact technology has on learning and the changes that will be necessary to improve instruction (Townley and Parsell, 2004).

Improving Instruction

Instructors are the key to fostering a learning-oriented environment because "students' conceptions of learning are mediated by how well professors communicate their expectations to students, foster higher order learning in their classes, and evaluate it" (Donald, 1997, p. 110). Unfortunately, most postsecondary education faculty have not been trained in effective instruction or assessment (Stiggins, 2002). A lack of familiarity with how to assess student learning and individual achievement when students have worked with others, for instance, leads instructors to classify collaboration as a dishonest act. Many experts suggest, however, that collaboration is a way to enhance learning (Association of American Colleges and Universities, 2002; Bruffee, 1984; Donald, 1997; Kuh and others, 2005). Although it is admittedly more difficult to coordinate and evaluate than independent work, students have always and probably always will seek out others for help when they are struggling to learn or complete a difficult assignment. Thus, to enhance the integrity of instruction for learning, instructors should learn to "harness the powerful educative force of peer influence that [has] been—and largely still is—ignored and hence wasted by traditional forms of education" (Bruffee, 1984, p. 638).

Improved instruction for the learning-oriented environment has several characteristics, including focusing on the learner and learning outcomes, clarifying learning goals as connected to each assignment, using assessments that focus on higher-order thinking rather than rote memorization, regularly soliciting student feedback on instruction, holding students to high standards and avoiding busy-work assignments, embracing the power of technology to evolve learning tasks, stressing inquiry and facilitating engagement and the application of learning to real-world problems, and a faculty acting more as coaches and mentors than as ultimate experts (American Association of Colleges and Universities, 2002; Donald, 1997; Guskin, 1994). Although some changes to instruction are more difficult, rather simple changes can improve "some of the classroom environment dimensions associated with cheating attitudes and behavior, for example, moving around in the classroom and mixing with students, being friendly and asking students about their welfare, using more group work and praise to reinforce student contributions, encouraging student participation" (Pulvers and Diekhoff, 1999, p. 496).

Questions could be added to course evaluations about the teaching and learning norms of the classroom. Questions could be asked about faculty behaviors (does she consistently arrives on time?) and student behaviors (do students use unauthorized aids, copy, or engage in some other act of cheating during examinations?). The results of the course evaluations could be used to help faculty see the connections between their conduct and that of their students and suggest how they could improve their teaching. Overall, the teaching and learning strategy highlights changes in instruction, assignments, and assessment as more viable ways to enhance academic integrity than attempts to control and legislate students' conduct (Introna, Hayes, Blair, and Wood, 2003; Townley and Parsell, 2004). Faculty cannot possibly improve instruction without institutional support, however.

Enhancing Institutional Support

The teaching and learning strategy seeks to develop clear institutional support for integrity in the teaching and learning environment. Students and instructors cannot change their conduct and ways of interacting with one another without external support from the institution. Students and instructors must see that integrity is something "to which leaders pay attention, measure, and control" (Whitly and Keith-Spiegel, 2001, p. 339), which means not just integrity of students but also the integrity of teachers, researchers, and administrators. Human, political, monetary, and structural support should be given to departments that make efforts to enhance a learning-oriented environment and instructors' teaching abilities. Campus leadership should work with faculty, staff, and students to explore student and faculty attitudes toward student cheating (a common activity in the integrity strategy) but move beyond it to also "examine entrenched ideas about learning and teaching and attempt to change attitudes" (Donald, 1997, p. 132). Entrenched ideas about learning as the production of a right answer and teaching as the evaluation of that right answer may inhibit students and faculty from changing the ways in which they interact in the classroom, for example.

Campus administration can show support for teaching and teaching development by rewarding and honoring good teaching, preparing future faculty to be effective teachers, increasing dialogue and attention to teaching, and reducing obstacles to an enhanced focus on teaching (Donald, 1997). Academic integrity should be a significant component of teaching support. Institutions can support integrity in learning by purposefully and formally introducing students to the expectations and learning outcomes of the academic community, establishing a writing and learning center that can work closely with students and faculty in developing writing and information literacy in students, reducing institutional dependency on large lecture examination-based classes, reducing institutional dependency on adjunct lecturers, and increasing opportunities for students to develop mentoring and apprentice relationships with graduate students and faculty.

Reducing Institutional Constraints

The teaching and learning strategy also encourages the examination and removal of "institutional constraints" (Arnstine, 1978) that impair or inhibit teaching and learning and the desired conduct of students in their academic endeavors. Such institutional constraints as administrative systems, educational bureaucracies, and standardized testing methods shape the nature of the college student. The teaching and learning strategy suggests that these institutional constraints be examined for their impact on the integrity of the teaching and learning environment.

The institutional constraints shaping the contemporary context for academic conduct were discussed previously, but in general campuses may want to examine obstacles that constrain faculty members' ability to frequently interact with students throughout the learning process, including taking the time to meet the students who are struggling with writing or with the material, developing their teaching skills, and creating meaningful assessment tasks (Carroll and Appleton, 2001; Guskin, 1994; McCabe and Pavela, n.d.). Campuses could also consider removing obstacles that prevent faculty members from addressing academic misconduct in their classes such as lack of proctoring and grading support, cumbersome policies, and negative effects on teaching evaluations. For example, Whitley and Keith-Spiegel (2001) suggest that academic departments be given authority to ignore "the lowest evaluation class in which an accusation of dishonesty was made" (p. 334).

Several obstacles could be removed to create an environment in which it is easier for students to conduct their academic work with integrity. Research has found that students engage in academic misconduct because they lack clear guidelines on how to conduct their academic work, feel that situations are out of their control, fail to see the importance of integrity in learning, continue practices perfected in secondary education, use all available resources to complete their work, and react to their instructors' actions (Granitz and Loewy, 2007; McCabe, 1992; Roig, 2001). Many institutions have not yet resolved internal inconsistencies that invite students to engage in behaviors that may be labeled as misconduct.

One of the most common internal inconsistencies I have seen in both practice and research is the prohibition against the use of unauthorized aid in the face of the prevalent availability of old examinations, lab reports, and essays for students' use. Another is the simultaneous encouragement of and prohibition against collaboration (Drinan, 1999). Institutions could begin to reduce the potency of these obstacles by openly and clearly addressing the proper use of resources such as old examinations and assignments, the Internet, friends, tutors, and parents (Carroll and Appleton, 2001; Granitz and Loewy, 2007). In addition, students could be better acculturated into the expectations of the academy and be taught the conventions of their future disciplines and professions, and assessments could be revised and individualized more regularly (Carroll and Appleton, 2001; Introna, Hayes, Blair, and Wood, 2003).

Assessment and the Teaching and Learning Strategy

As evidenced in the four goals previously described, the teaching and learning strategy calls for a more direct and explicit link between assessment and academic integrity. When it is the academic misconduct of students in question, campus officials and faculty are primarily concerned with the negative impact on two aspects of the educative process—learning and fair evaluation of students' work. If assessment "is the process of evaluating student learning and development to improve learning, instruction, and program effectiveness" (Donald, 1997, p. 161), then clearly assessment can be a significant component of the teaching and learning strategy for ensuring integrity in academic work. Until this point, organizational approaches have focused on punishing and correcting student behavior thought to undermine valid assessments. The teaching and learning strategy suggests, however, that the assessment mechanisms themselves as well as teachers' conduct and the organizational and institutional environments need to be considered in a comprehensive approach to academic integrity (Introna, Hayes, Blair, and Wood, 2003).

In their practice guide to plagiarism, Carroll and Appleton (2001) argue that changing assessments, thoroughly considering learning outcomes, creating individualized tasks, integrating assessment tasks, and setting a range of assessment tasks are good practices to ensure the integrity of academic work. It is the responsibility of the teacher and the institution to ensure that assessment tasks are relevant and learning oriented and that students understand how the assessments are linked to learning outcomes and how each assessment supports another to build knowledge and skills. Introna, Hayes, Blair, and Wood (2003) also discuss the importance of helping students connect assessment exercises to their self-development and learning; otherwise, students feel alienated from the process and believe that cheating is "morally justifiable" (p. 45). Postsecondary education institutions cannot be concerned with student actions undermining the learning and assessment process unless they are also concerned with ensuring the assessments themselves are fair, transparent, and valid.

Stiggins (2002) writes about the assessment crisis that focuses on assessment *of* learning and neglects assessment *for* learning. Stiggins argues that the current focus on assessing how much students have learned may induce some students to work harder and learn more but may also induce other students to give up or, I would argue, cheat. Assessment for learning may help students engage in their academic work with greater integrity by:

Helping them to build *"confidence* in themselves as learners and to take responsibility for their own learning . . .

Engaging students in *regular self-assessment,* with standards held constant so that students can watch themselves grow over time and thus feel in charge of their own success . . . [and]

Actively involving students in *communicating* with their teacher and their families about their achievement status and improvement" (Stiggins, 2002, p. 762).

Without this attention to the assessment and learning process as well as to the way in which students engage in their academic work, academic conduct may be misdiagnosed as an ethical failure rather than, sometimes, a failure to teach or a failure to learn.

Accreditation and the Teaching and Learning Strategy

The teaching and learning strategy also calls for a more direct link with the process of accreditation. Each institution must be responsive to an accrediting commission, depending on its geographic region, which can sanction educational institutions for serious noncompliance with their standards. The purposes of accreditation, according to the Western Association of Schools and Colleges (2001), are in part to assure the public that institutions are performing with integrity, improve the teaching and learning process, and improve educational quality and institutional performance.

The purposes of accreditation, then, seem aligned with the purposes of the teaching and learning strategy to enhance academic integrity, which underscores the multidimensional character of academic integrity. If students' academic work can be seen as a part of the standards for accreditation (which for the Western Association of Schools and Colleges are defining institutional purposes and achieving educational objectives through core functions, developing and applying resources and organizational structures to ensure sustainability, and creating an organization committed to learning and improvement), it may highlight the connections among the conduct of students, faculty, researchers, and administrators as well as between student academic conduct and the organizational, institutional, and societal dimensions of the issue.

Structures and Policies in the Teaching and Learning Strategy

Although the goals of the teaching and learning strategy focus on the macrolevel of enhancing the teaching and learning environment, a local academic integrity initiative is still necessary, including the implementation of structures and policies that address academic misconduct. This section describes how structures and policies in the teaching and learning strategy may be different from those that fall under the rule compliance and integrity strategies.

Organizational Structures

In a rule compliance and integrity strategy, student academic misconduct is the responsibility of those offices responsible for the management and oversight of the conduct code, academic integrity policy, honor code, or modified honor code. Institutions with traditional honor codes tend to have a student-run system that handles the communication of the honor principle and the coordination of the reporting and adjudicating functions (such as the Honor Committee at the University of Virginia). Institutions with modified honor codes or integrity policies tend to employ one of two structures: (1) a judicial affairs office, which handles all student misconduct (for example, the Office of Student Conduct at the University of Maryland) or (2) a discrete administrative office that handles only academic conduct violations (for instance, the Honor and Integrity System office at Kansas State University). Whichever form the structure takes, the student misconduct office is most often disconnected from the offices that deal with the integrity of teaching, research, or administration.

Under a teaching and learning strategy, the structures may be decidedly different because the involvement of faculty and other academic staff should be made paramount (Buchanan and Beckham, 2006). This shifting of the balance from an emphasis on student affairs to a triumvirate of faculty–academic affairs–student affairs can do much to decrease a focus on conduct and increase teaching and learning considerations. To reflect this shift, the academic integrity program could be situated in an existing structure that focuses on teaching and learning such as a teaching and learning development center or the library. Or perhaps an academic integrity office could be created that focuses broadly on the integrity of students, faculty, researchers, administrators, and the institution.

The best structure is one that is aligned with institutional characteristics but also positioned in a way that symbolizes the primacy of the teaching and learning environment and the importance of integrity for all organizational members. This symbolism may best be realized by having faculty rather than judicial affairs officers as key leaders of the academic integrity initiative, although representatives from across the community need to be involved in realizing the vision of the teaching and learning strategy.

Organizational Policies

Codes of academic conduct for all organizational members can be useful in articulating expectations, responsibilities, and norms, especially in diverse institutions where the likelihood of ethical dilemmas looms large because of multiple competing interests and goals (Bray and Del Favero, 2004). In such environments, the clear articulation of norms helps to guide people in their decision making, no matter the level or scope of their responsibilities (Braxton, Bayer, and Noseworthy, 2002).

The very factor that makes codes useful, however, also undermines their effectiveness—the private and autonomous nature of teaching and learning (Whicker and Kronenfeld, 1994). Because academic work is largely private and filled with competing priorities, the educational institution must be able to depend on individual integrity and a commitment to follow institutional policies (Shils, 1983). Park (2004) argued this point: "the academic enterprise is rooted in a culture of integrity, founded on honesty and mutual trust, and the university should expect all of its members (staff and students) to respect and uphold these core values at all times, in everything we do at, for, and in the name of the institution" (p. 297). Therefore, even in the teaching and learning strategy, disciplinary and integrity policies are necessary. These policies, however, will differ from those traditionally found in organizational strategies to stop students from cheating.

Reframe Academic Integrity as Standards of Practice. Rather than perpetuating the in loco parentis model of controlling students' academic conduct, which is common in the rule compliance and integrity strategies, the teaching and learning strategy reframes academic conduct rules as standards of practice, and it does so for all institutional members. Thus, on campuses following this strategy, traditional student academic integrity policies could be replaced by a document that addresses academic standards of practice and details expectations for all parties in the teaching and learning process—faculty, students, and teaching assistants. These standards could be written in a similar language and style to those common in other professions such as law, medicine, or engineering, thereby functioning not just to guide faculty and student behaviors for the enhancement of the teaching and learning environment but also to socialize students to the expectations and normative understandings of their future professions.

Distinguish Between Fraud and Failure. Policies in the teaching and learning strategy may differentiate between acts that are dishonest or fraudulent and those that emerge out of learning struggles, failure to complete the assignment in expected ways, or teaching mishaps. Fraud undermines or thwarts university functions of teaching (learning), service, and research; it is intentional deception for self-gain. Students commit academic fraud when they intentionally misrepresent their knowledge and abilities (thereby subverting the purpose of evaluation) or pretend to engage in the process of the assignment or exam but do not (subverting the purpose of learning). Examples of student academic fraud include submitting a purchased or borrowed paper as one's own; arranging for or serving as an examination proxy; obtaining an advanced copy of a test, assignment, or examination; and taking another student's assignment or exam and using it as one's own. Researchers commit fraud when they intentionally misrepresent their research findings or pretend to have performed a study when they have not. Administrators commit fraud when they alter submitted grades to misrepresent student successes or promise attention to learning but then approve classes with extraordinarily large teacher-student ratios. Fraud in any form should be considered unacceptable in the institution and disciplined accordingly to discourage rampant corruption.

Nonfraudulent behaviors, on the other hand, are represented by the individual's mistake or inability to follow expected or normative procedures, rules, or guidelines for a particular assignment. This distinction is common when the conduct in question is that of the faculty-researcher (Ronning, Anderson, de Vries, and Martinson, 2007). Howard (1995) argued that such a distinction must also be extended to student conduct. Failure or misbehavior may not always subvert learning, as in the case of unauthorized collaboration, use of unauthorized aids, or even "copying and pasting" because learning is relative. Failure, however, can indicate a breach of standards that needs to be addressed in some way in an effort to teach students about the importance of community and professional standards. For example, insufficient citation and excessive repetition in students' writing would not be punished in the same way as fraud or plagiarism but responded to pedagogically in ways that would advance the student as a writer (Howard, 2000b; Maruca, 2001).

Acknowledge Conflicting Notions of Authorship, Information, and Knowledge. Institutional policies in a teaching and learning approach would acknowledge the multiple perspectives that coexist about authorship, information, and knowledge. Positively acknowledging the collaborative nature of writing from which citation and attribution rules are partly derived is different from negatively characterizing a student as immoral and dishonest when he or she does not acknowledge the ideas and text borrowed from others (Howard, 1995;

Maruca, 2001). Critics of the dominant organizational strategies often "view plagiarism as a problem in the development of 'voice,' a reflection of a student's lack of confidence in his or her own opinions and authority, or a misunderstanding of the very purposes of academic writing. Because they see plagiarism as a complex learning issue, these educators question the morality of 'prosecuting' students for their ignorance or lack of ability" (Maruca, 2001, p. 1129).

In my own experience, students are much more willing to accept responsibility for violating standards of practice (such as improper citation) than they are for accepting the label of cheater or plagiarist. The accusation of immorality is a defamation of character, one most people would be unwilling to accept and one that may not be productive in an educative environment. In acknowledging coexisting notions of knowledge and information, students can be brought into the discussion about preferred social conventions and professional ethics rather than polarize them as the moral enemy. This alternate view seems most prevalent among writing instructors whose role it is to develop students as writers, although I have also experienced many writing instructors who function as plagiarism police.

To move on the issue of academic integrity, it may be helpful to acknowledge the multiple perceptions and contradictions in the very concepts themselves *while* establishing and maintaining standards. According to Bruffee (1984), "We must perform as conservators *and* agents of change, as custodians of prevailing community values *and* as agents of social transition and re-acculturation" (p. 650). Educators who clearly and consistently articulate the accepted ways of doing academic work in a particular discipline as well as struggle with accepting and incorporating new ways will keep learning, rather than cheating, at the forefront.

Emphasize the Roles and Responsibilities of Other Parties. Academic integrity policies in the teaching and learning strategy would also better emphasize the roles and responsibilities of faculty, academic departments, schools or colleges, and the institution as a whole. Disciplinary sanctions would be applied in very specific cases where the student seems to be trending down a dangerous road of ethical noncompliance. But not all transgressions would be predetermined as morally corrupt. Cases of plagiarism, for example, would be specifically assessed to determine whether the problem is misconduct or a novice writer's struggle with an assignment.

In addition, the institution would be responsible for incorporating a focus on the development of students as writers, thinkers, and ethical citizens into the core curriculum rather than reserving it as a response to misconduct. Policies would also require faculty to clearly explicate course expectations, learning outcomes, and connections between assessments and learning. Thus, when students are charged with academic misconduct, the syllabus and assignment instructions would be examined to determine whether a reasonable person could understand course requirements and the purpose of the assignments; if not, then the student's conduct may be determined to be a result of misunderstanding rather than misconduct.

Summary

The repeated reports of misconduct on the part of students, if true, may undermine the integrity of the academic enterprise. Yet beyond few cases of outright fraud, many of the behaviors defined as misconduct (such as unauthorized collaboration, use of unauthorized aid, and plagiarism) may be less an outcome of immorality and more an outgrowth of the forces shaping different notions of knowledge, information, and the role of the academy. The dominance of rule compliance and integrity strategies may strain the teaching and learning environment and actually interfere with the goals of academic integrity because they do not consider these forces or the multiple dimensions of academic misconduct. This section reviewed a third possible strategy that addresses academic misconduct by focusing on ensuring that students are learning rather than stopping them from cheating. This strategy includes the disciplining of misconduct or fraud and the development of students' ethical reasoning but expands organizational responses to include the improvement of instruction, the removal of obstacles to integrity, and the enhancement of institutional support for academic integrity. Exhibit 4 summarizes the teaching and learning strategy. The next section further discusses the multiple practice and research possibilities implicated by the teaching and learning strategy.

EXHIBIT 4
Summary of the Teaching and Learning Strategy

Characterization of the Problem or Issue

Academic integrity is an issue for all members of the community, shaped by student, faculty, researcher, and administrator conduct as well as by organizational, institutional, and societal forces.

Characterization of the Actors

Members of the academic community face difficult ethical choices on a daily basis and may lack the appropriate skills, information, or support to choose the actions that support the integrity of the teaching and learning environment.

Characterization of the Solution

Academic integrity can be enhanced by communicating expectations and guidelines for conduct, offering opportunities for the development of ethical reasoning skills, eliminating obstacles to teaching and learning, and reducing obstacles to decision making that aligns with institutional integrity.

Common Strategy Questions

What norms, values, and assumptions in the organizational culture (and subcultures) may support, and what ones may detract from, teaching and learning?

What institutional structures constrain faculty and students from engaging in their roles and work with integrity?

What are some of the ways in which technology, diversity, and academic capitalism may be changing the ways in which our faculty teach and our students learn?

How do we fold processes and education about responsible ethical conduct into a broader teaching and learning strategy in ways that are not disjointed or fragmented?

Primary Organizational Actions

Academic integrity is made a primary strategic objective for the institution (rather than as a student affairs or student issue).

Consultations and workshops are made available to faculty to help them develop the skills for ensuring the integrity of the teaching and learning process in their classes.

The "one size fits all" approach to education and remediation is replaced with multiple interventions that focus on enhancing learning and integrity in academic work. Ethics workshops are augmented with skill development programs that help students with writing, time management, or other problems interfering with their ability to learn.

An academic socialization freshman seminar is created that helps to orient students to their role as student in the academic community.

Changes are made to the tenure and promotion practices to ensure faculty work on teaching and learning integrity is appropriately rewarded.

Transparency and accountability are enhanced at all organizational levels so that student academic conduct does not receive harsher or greater attention than misconduct at other levels.

Common Organizational Structures

The academic integrity office is positioned outside of student judicial affairs in a division or department associated with teaching and learning on campus (for example, under the chief academic affairs officer or with a center for teaching and learning) or as part of a larger unit that addresses ethics and integrity at all levels from student, faculty, and researcher to administration.

An academic integrity policy is established that covers guidelines and expectations for all members of the academy to ensure the integrity of teaching and learning, distinct from codes of conduct that cover such behaviors as drinking, sexual harassment, and discrimination.

An integrity committee composed of students, faculty, and administrators serves to consider all issues that affect the integrity of the teaching and learning environment, from individual conduct to forces in the organizational, institutional, and societal dimension such as technology and institutional constraints.

Recommendations for Practice and Research

A TEACHING AND LEARNING STRATEGY for enhancing academic integrity allows for a robust organizational approach that situates academic conduct in the teaching and learning imperative of the twenty-first-century postsecondary education campus. Although the appeal of the rule compliance and integrity strategies cannot be ignored, attempts to address a complex issue like academic integrity naturally resort to the lowest common denominator, that is, the conduct of students. It is not only simple to frame the issue in terms of stopping students from cheating: the primary disciplinary and developmental methods of the rule compliance and integrity strategies are more practical and easily implemented by student affairs professionals.

The shift to the more inclusive teaching and learning strategy calls for post secondary education institutions to stop focusing on "how do we stop students from cheating?" and begin to focus on "how do we ensure students are learning?" Although the second question still calls for defining and enforcing behavioral standards and supporting students' ethical development, it does so in a macrolens that also requires changes in the institution beyond changes to the student body. In other words, the "primary responsibility for the problem shifts from the student to the academic and the institution" (Leask, 2006, p. 189). This strategy is admittedly more challenging to implement. It requires more extensive involvement on the part of faculty and academic affairs staff as well as changes to the teaching and learning environment. Several recommendations for practice provided in the previous section and this one should provide some assistance to campuses interested in the strategy. This section ends with some possibilities to expand knowledge and enhance practice through further research.

Recommendations for Practice

The previous section offered several practical recommendations for initiating a teaching and learning strategy such as creating new structures and policies and linking academic integrity with assessment and accreditation. This section contains five additional recommendations for those interested in positioning academic integrity as a teaching and learning imperative.

Assess Your Organizational Strategy

Postsecondary education institutions interested in exploring their strategy for enhancing academic integrity (in its broadest sense) may want to assess currently employed strategies. Is discipline, development, or pedagogy paramount in conversations about students' academic misconduct? Is students' academic misconduct considered in tandem with other student misbehaviors or in tandem with teachers', researchers', and administrators' conduct? Are sanctions for misconduct harsh, resulting in removal from the institution, or are they developmental or educational? Who is involved in conversations and efforts directed toward enhancing academic integrity? Are students, faculty, or student affairs professionals responsible for implementing and enforcing the policy and procedures? Although an organizational strategy assessment instrument has yet to be developed, the exhibits summarizing and comparing the rule compliance, integrity, and teaching and learning strategies could be used for guidance.

Build Strong Campus Partnerships

If academic integrity is to be considered synonymous with institutional integrity, it must be attended to by all members of the postsecondary education institution rather than only students or student affairs and judicial officers. Faculty, staff, and students can be brought together to talk about academic integrity, enhance a learning-oriented environment, improve instruction, remove obstacles, and enhance institutional support for acting with integrity.

Others have written about the importance of student affairs professionals and librarians partnering to improve academic integrity education for students (Swartz, Carlisle, and Uyeki, 2007). Librarians, staff in teaching development centers, tutors, writing center directors, academic advisors, faculty senators, provosts, ethics personnel, and student affairs professionals can all add insight and perspective on enhancing academic integrity. Strong partnerships that transcend traditional organizational boundaries may be one of the most critical and yet most unrealized components for developing robust organizational responses to issues of integrity. These partnerships are also critical to ensure that there is ongoing dialogue about academic integrity that spans the breadth and multiple dimensions of the issue.

Enhance Student Socialization into the Academy

Both the rule compliance and integrity strategies assume that students understand and share the values of the institution. Thus, new students are often not fully enculturated into the rules and norms of the academy in those colleges and universities that employ these dominant organizational strategies. Most of the students attending colleges and universities, however, will not become permanent academics, and so it is unlikely that they will understand or share underlying values such as the pursuit of truth or the protection of intellectual property. Moreover, students attend college for their own purposes (for example, to advance in a career), so they may be unduly pressed to put the faculty's or institution's interests ahead of their own. Yet orientation sessions for new students seldom deal with these conflicting notions or interests, replacing this ethical development with the preaching of the importance of honor and integrity, complete with pledge-signing ceremonies and motivational speakers.

Orientations for new students that focus predominantly on student life and extracurricular activities need to be revised to highlight academic culture. It does not mean tagging an honor code–signing ceremony onto the traditional social orientation but fundamentally altering orientation to provide academic socialization. Such a requirement may even require a semester or year-long freshman seminar. Although its importance has been mentioned for students who speak English as a second language or international students (Kuehn, Stanwyck, and Holland, 1990), it seems imperative for all incoming students whose K–12 educational experience may have differed dramatically from what is expected in university or college. Brown and Howell (2001), for example, found that warning students of the hazards of "cheating" makes no imprint on their beliefs, whereas an educative statement about the norms and expectations for academic work does increase students' perceptions of the seriousness of behaviors that undermine the teaching and learning environment.

Clarify Standards of Professional Conduct

Despite, or perhaps because of, the multidimensional nature of academic misconduct, the need remains for clearly explicated standards of conduct. As mentioned earlier, publicized and accountable standards of practice help organizational members make decisions in the face of complex problems and ethical dilemmas. Much of the current talk of academic integrity, however, deflates all the varied reasons for standards and discipline into a statement against dishonesty or dishonor. As one example, the University of Virginia's honor system states that "by today's standard, an honor offense is defined as an intentional act of lying, cheating or stealing [that] warrants permanent dismissal from the University." In this sense, violations of academic conduct standards are treated in the same way as violations of criminal or civil laws, and acts such as unauthorized collaboration and copying and pasting are considered lying, cheating, or stealing.

In the teaching and learning strategy, standards for professional conduct are important because they help to protect the integrity of the teaching and learning environment, clearly articulate expectations so actors understand behavioral boundaries, and clarify ambiguous and vague terms (such as "collaboration" and "authorship"). The importance of these standards is not necessarily to declare someone a liar, cheat, or thief but to ensure that students (and faculty) understand how they can fulfill all their roles and responsibilities.

Link Academic Integrity to Institutional Integrity

The teaching and learning strategy suggests that academic integrity be considered in the context of institutional integrity rather than in the context of student misbehavior. One of the most effective ways to make that link is to have the university president or chancellor rather than the judicial affairs or student life administrator speak to the issue (Alschuler and Blimling, 1995). To link academic integrity to institutional integrity, postsecondary education organizations can also develop a list of "red flags," situations that may be susceptible to the corruption of teaching and learning (Hallak and Poisson, 2007).

What might be some of these red flags? Campuses can investigate whether the majority of student academic misconduct occurs in large classes or a certain department or program. Large classes are not conducive environments for undergraduate learning or the mentoring relationships between faculty and students that may be necessary for institutional integrity (Armentrout, 1979). Is there a lack of faculty reporting of academic misconduct on campus? Are students complaining about teaching or the educational process, using them as "excuses" for academic misconduct? Is there a specific type of student being reported for misconduct? Are there tremendous pressures on faculty to produce research without an equal release of teaching time? Are departments being pressured to increase the number of enrolled students without corresponding institutional support? Does the institution boast a quality undergraduate education and then manage large student populations with the use of undergraduates as teaching assistants? Answering questions such as these can begin to pinpoint underlying assumptions or tensions that may be contributing to academic misconduct. Asking these questions can also serve to broaden the discussion of academic misconduct beyond the culpability of students.

Contrary to what many have argued, institutional integrity does not rest in the hands of the student body alone; rather, "our integrity rests on how we treat our students, our colleagues, our staff, our board, and the parents of our students. It is inherent in our policies, our exceptions to our policies, and every aspect of our daily functioning as an institution of postsecondary education" (Barr, 1987, p. 2). Institutional integrity, especially for those institutions that claim a focus on undergraduate education, is tied fundamentally to the integrity of the teaching and learning environment. Thus, a teaching and learning approach directly connects students' academic conduct to the ways in which students learn and faculty teach—a consideration that has remained in the periphery of the concerns of most universities (Bok, 1986).

Recommendations for Research

The teaching and learning strategy argued in this monograph has not been thoroughly explored in practice or research. The opportunities for further research are numerous and exciting; only a few of them are suggested here.

Study, Characterize, and Catalogue Organizational Strategies

Research is needed to further elucidate the characteristics, goals, and outcomes of the rule compliance, integrity, and teaching and learning strategies. Several survey studies provide an initial picture of organizational activities and approaches (Aaron, 1992; Bertram Gallant and Drinan, 2006; Bush, 2000), and a few other studies have more deeply explored individual organizational efforts (Bertram Gallant, 2006). We need more qualitative studies that can study and characterize organizational strategies for enhancing academic integrity. These studies can be used to construct surveys to catalogue strategies nationwide and around the world as well as to develop instruments to help institutions assess their own strategy and move from rule compliance or integrity strategies to a teaching and learning strategy.

Explore Connections Between Faculty and Student Misconduct

An abundance of research is available on student and faculty perceptions of, attitudes toward, and self-reported actions in relation to academic misconduct. On the other hand, information is lacking on the connections between the misconduct of faculty and that of students and how teaching and learning dynamics affect academic conduct. Preliminary research could maintain the survey methodology but go beyond perceptions and attitudes to determining when students engage in certain behaviors. Such studies could reveal possible correlations between student conduct and environmental factors.

A study by Roberts and Rabinowitz (1992) provides one research model. In this study, students on three different state university campuses were presented variations of a case study in which a student copies from his peers during an examination. The case study varied only on four variables: copying for survival, poor instructional environment, opportunity, and intentionality. The respondents were asked to assess, on a scale from low to high, whether the student in the case study cheated, whether the student did something wrong, and whether the student should be punished. The authors found that students were less likely to view the student as morally wrong if the instructor or the class were perceived to be unrewarding, arbitrary, or unfairly difficult. Roberts and Rabinowitz (1992) concluded that more research is needed to understand "how people (both students and faculty) perceive cheating and its seriousness . . . [because] if cheating is perceived as less serious because instructors teach poorly and give unfair exams, then the primary solution is not to crack down on cheating but to improve instruction and fairness" (p. 189). After additional such survey research, experimental studies could be conducted to test the correlations between student and faculty conduct and suggest improvements to the teaching and learning environment.

Investigate Teaching and Learning Norms

The work of Braxton, Bayer, and others on classroom norms can be further extended to suggest possible connections between faculty and student conduct and the normative behaviors in a department, school, college, or institution that may undermine integrity. For example, research routinely demonstrates that engineering and business students self-report more academic misconduct than other students (McCabe, 2005a). Is it because engineering and business students are more honest about their behaviors or because they cheat more? If they cheat more than other students, why? Is it a function of class size, instructor methods, norms of the disciplines? An investigation of teaching and learning norms in these disciplines and a comparison with other disciplines could shed light on this phenomenon.

Study Connections Between Academic Misconduct and Learning

Academic integrity writers and researchers have been arguing for years that student academic misconduct is problematic because of its capacity to undermine learning. Evidence is lacking to support this statement, however. In fact, because the research also shows that students are more likely to engage in unauthorized collaboration or "cheat" on menial assignments, some evidence may suggest that students are more likely to break the rules when they do not see a negative effect on their learning. The need for such research has been advocated for a number of years (Houston, 1976). Several questions should be investigated: Does the perceived opportunity to cheat affect the amount learned? Does the amount learned affect the amount of cheating? Do students cheat more on assignments determined to be unrelated to learning? And do students engage in unauthorized behaviors in an attempt to increase their learning? Both experimental and qualitative studies are needed to enhance an understanding of the relationship between students' academic misconduct and learning.

Study Strains on the Teaching and Learning Environment

This monograph suggests that inattention to the multidimensional nature of the issue and the forces shaping twenty-first-century education strains the teaching and learning environment. Much research is needed to examine the impact of the dominant rule compliance and integrity strategies. One possible area for research is how faculty and students perceive their relationship and act out their roles on campuses that subscribe to the rule compliance strategy. Ethnographic research conducted in classrooms and with students and faculty as they engage in their work could significantly enhance our understanding of the impact on the faculty-student relationship when the focus is on stopping students from cheating. Magolda's model of self-authorship (1999) could be applied to understand how the rule compliance and integrity strategies enhance or diminish students' learning and development of self-authorship. The work by Appel-Silbaugh (2007) on the self-authorship of honor council members may provide a useful starting point. If institutions exist that employ a teaching and learning strategy, the distinctive challenges and strains it precipitates could also be studied.

Summary

The call for postsecondary education institutions to shift their focus from asking "how can we stop students from cheating?" to asking "how can we ensure students are learning?" is bold and perhaps presumptuous when considered on the surface. "Surely," the response might be, "our institutions already do their best to ensure that students are learning. But when it comes right down to it, acting with academic integrity is students' responsibility, not ours."

The intent of this monograph is not to displace responsibility for students' learning from students to teachers, academic administrators, or student affairs professionals but to acknowledge the complexity of the academic misconduct phenomenon that cannot be fully explained by the internal dimension or student character. But no matter how committed educators are to working in a way that facilitates learning, students who choose to engage in behaviors that subvert learning, undermine fair assessments, and commit outright fraud will always be around. This monograph supports the call of earlier works to respond to such behaviors through both disciplinary and developmental methods (Dannells, 1997; Whitley and Keith-Spiegel, 2001).

At the same time, this monograph urges educators and administrators to consider that if academic misconduct is as prevalent and insidious on college campuses as suggested, then the rule compliance and integrity strategies may not be sufficient responses. Postsecondary education institutions and arguably elementary and secondary systems as well should continue to enforce standards of conduct and teach students the importance of ethics, integrity, and honor. The history and multidimensional nature of academic misconduct suggest that these efforts should be coordinated with those intended to enhance the integrity of the work done by faculty as teachers, researchers, and administrators. Students should hear and see evidence that colleges and universities are concerned about institutional integrity, not simply the integrity of the learners. To ask "how can we ensure students are learning?" centralizes students as learners rather than offenders and faculty as teachers rather than police officers. To ask "how can we ensure students are learning?" invites strategies that facilitate organizational and institutional change in ways that improve instruction, remove obstacles to learning, and enhance the support for the teaching and learning environment. In the end, this monograph calls for academic integrity to become part of the teaching and learning imperative that is gaining strength on college and university campuses around the world.

References

Aaron, R. M. (1992, Winter). Student academic dishonesty: Are collegiate institutions addressing the issue? *NASPA Journal,* (2), 107–113.

Akst, D. (1987, November 18). Novel approach: Video cheating emerges as the latest student shortcut to reading. *Wall Street Journal.* Retrieved October 21, 2006, from ProQuest Historical Newspapers.

Allmendinger, D. F., Jr. (1973). The dangers of antebellum student life. *Journal of Social History, 7*(1), 75–85.

Alschuler, A. S., and Blimling, G. S. (1995). Curbing epidemic cheating through systematic change. *College Teaching, 43*(4), 123–125.

Amsden, D. (1977). Fraud in academe. *Phi Kappa Phi Journal, 57*(1), 37–44.

Angell, R. C. (1928). *The campus: A study of contemporary undergraduate life in the American university.* New York: D. Appelton & Company.

Anglen, R. (2006, October 15). College leaders' trips scrutinized—pricey hotels, meals common; Mesa community defends global outreach efforts. *Arizona Republic.* Retrieved March 15, 2007, from www.newsbank.com.

Appel-Silbaugh, C. D. (2007). *Acting out integrity and honor: Student honor council cultural influence on members' development.* Doctoral dissertation, University of Maryland, College Park.

Apple, M. (2003). The state and the politics of knowledge. In M. W. Apple (Ed.), *The state and the politics of knowledge* (pp. 1–24). New York: RoutledgeFalmer.

Armentrout, W. D. (1979). Neglected values in postsecondary education. *Journal of Higher Education, 50*(4), 361–367.

Arnstine, D. (1978). Improving instruction: Reform the institution, not the faculty. *Liberal Education, 64*(3), 266–277.

Association of American Colleges and Universities. (2002). *Greater expectations: A new vision for learning as a nation goes to college.* Washington, DC: Association of American Colleges and Universities.

Association of American Colleges and Universities. (2004). *Our students' best work: A framework for accountability worthy of our mission.* Washington, DC: Association of American Colleges and Universities.

Astin, A. (1993). *Postsecondary education and the concept of community.* Fifteenth David Dodds Henry Lecture, University of Illinois, Champaign, IL.

Astin, A. (1996). Involvement in learning revisited: Lessons we have learned. *Journal of College Student Development, 37*(2), 123–134.

Baird, J. S., Jr. (1980). Current trends in college cheating. *Psychology in the Schools, 17*(4), 515–522.

Barnes, W. F. (1975). Test information: An application of the economics of search. *Journal of Economic Education, 7*(1), 28–33.

Barnett, D. C., and Dalton, J. C. (1981). Why college students cheat. *Journal of College Student Personnel, 22*(6), 545–551.

Barr, M. J. (1987). Individual and institutional integrity. *NASPA Journal, 24*(4), 2–5.

Barr, R. B., and Tagg, J. (1994, November/December). From teaching to learning: A new paradigm for undergraduate education. *Change,* 13–25.

Batson, T., and Bass, R. (1996). Teaching and learning in the computer age: Primacy of process. *Change, 28*(2), 42–47.

Bayer, A. E. (2004). Promulgating statements of student rights and responsibilities. In J. M. Braxton and A. E. Bayer (Eds.), *Addressing faculty and student classroom improprieties* (pp. 77–87). San Francisco: Jossey-Bass.

Beck, L., and Ajzen, I. (1991). Predicting dishonest actions using the theory of planned behavior. *Journal of Research in Personality, 25*(3), 285–301.

Becker, H. S., Geer, B., and Hughes, E. C. (1968). *Making the grade: The academic side of college life.* New York: Wiley.

Bellico, R. (1979). Postsecondary education: Crisis of expectations. *Educational Record, 60*(1), 93–98.

Berkowitz, A. D. (2005). An overview of the social norms approach. In L. C. Lederman and L. P. Stewart (Eds.), *Changing the culture of college drinking: A socially situated health communication campaign* (pp. 193–241). Cresskill, NJ: Hampton Press.

Bertram Gallant, T. (2006). Reconsidering academic dishonesty: A critical examination of a complex organizational problem. Doctoral dissertation, University of San Diego, 2006.

Bertram Gallant, T. (2007). The complexity of integrity culture change: A case study of a liberal arts college. *Review of Higher Education, 30*(4), 391–411.

Bertram Gallant, T., and Drinan, P. (2006). Institutionalizing academic integrity: Administrator perceptions and institutional actions. *NASPA Journal, 44*(1), 61–81.

Besvinick, S. L. (1983). Integrity and the future of the university. *Journal of Higher Education, 54*(5), 566–573.

Blizek, W. L. (2000). Ethics and the educational community. *Studies in Philosophy and Education, 19,* 241–251.

Boice, B. (1996). Classroom incivilities. *Research in Higher Education, 37*(4), 453–486.

Bok, D. (1986). *Higher learning.* Cambridge, MA: Harvard University Press.

Bok, D. (1990). *Universities and the future of America.* Durham, NC: Duke University Press.

Bok, D. (2003). *Universities in the marketplace: The commercialization of postsecondary education.* Princeton, NJ: Princeton University Press.

Bowden, D. (1996). Coming to terms: Plagiarism. *English Journal, 85*(4), 82–84.

Bowers, W. J. (1964). *Student dishonesty and its control in college*. New York: Bureau of Applied Social Research, Columbia University.

Bowers, W. J. (1968). Confronting college cheating. In C. W. Havice (Ed.), *Campus values* (pp. 73–87). New York: Scribner's.

Bowman, J. (2006). *Honor: A history*. New York: Encounter Books.

Boynton, R. S. (2001, May 27). Is honor up for grabs? *Washington Post*. Retrieved March 15, 2007, from www.newsbank.com.

Braxton, J. M., and Bayer, A. E. (1994). Perceptions of research misconduct and an analysis of their correlates. *Journal of Higher Education, 65*(3), 351–372.

Braxton, J. M., and Bayer, A. E. (1999). *Faculty misconduct in collegiate teaching*. Baltimore: Johns Hopkins University Press.

Braxton, J. M., and Bayer, A. E. (2004). Toward a code of conduct for undergraduate teaching. In J. M. Braxton and A. E. Bayer (Eds.), *Addressing faculty and student classroom improprieties* (pp. 47–55). San Francisco: Jossey-Bass.

Braxton, J. M., Bayer, A. E., and Noseworthy, J. A. (2002). Students as tenuous agents of social control of professorial misconduct. *Peabody Journal of Education, 77*(3), 101–124.

Braxton, J. M., and Mann, M. R. (2004). Incidence and student response to faculty teaching norm violations. In J. M. Braxton and A. E. Bayer (Eds.), *Addressing faculty and student classroom improprieties* (pp. 35–40). San Francisco: Jossey-Bass.

Bray, N. J., and Del Favero, M. (2004). Sociological explanations for faculty and student classroom incivilities. In J. M. Braxton and A. E. Bayer (Eds.), *Addressing faculty and student classroom improprieties* (pp. 9–19). San Francisco: Jossey-Bass.

Briggs, L.B.R. (1969). *College life: Essays reprinted from "School, College, and Character" and "Routine and Ideals."* Freeport, NY: Books for Libraries Press.

Brimble, M., and Stevenson-Clarke, P. (2006). Perceptions of the prevalence and seriousness of academic dishonesty in Australian universities. *Australian Educational Researcher, 32*(3), 19–44.

Brown, V. J., and Howell, M. E. (2001). The efficacy of policy statements on plagiarism: Do they change students' views? *Research in Higher Education, 42*(1), 103–118.

Bruffee, K. A. (1984). Collaborative learning and the "conversation of mankind." *College English, 46*(7), 635–652.

Bruster, B. (2004, Summer). Cut and paste from cyberspace: Competency's changing face. *Delta Kappa Gamma Bulletin*, 38–40.

Buchanan, J. H., and Beckham, J. C. (2006). A comprehensive academic honor policy for students: Ensuring due process, promoting academic integrity, and involving faculty. *Journal of College and University Law, 33*(1), 97–120.

Bunn, D. N., Caudill, S. B., and Gropper, D. M. (1992). Crime in the classroom: An economic analysis of undergraduate student cheating behavior. *Journal of Economic Education, 23*(3), 197–207.

Burrus, R. T., McGoldrick, K., and Schuhmann, P. W. (2007). Self-reports of student cheating: Does a definition of cheating matter? *Journal of Economic Education, 38*(1), 3–16.

Bush, D. K. (2000). *An examination of how selected colleges and universities promote student academic integrity.* Charlotte: University of Virginia.

Callahan, D. (1982). Should there be an academic code of ethics? *Journal of Higher Education, 53*(3), 335–344.

Callahan, D. (2004). *The cheating culture: Why more Americans are doing wrong to get ahead.* Orlando: Harcourt.

Carnegie Council on Policy Studies in Higher Education. (1979). *Fair practices in higher education: Rights and responsibilities of students and their colleges in a period of intensified competition for enrollments.* San Francisco: Jossey-Bass.

Carroll, J., and Appleton, J. (2001). *Plagiarism: A good practice guide.* Oxford, UK: Oxford Brookes University.

Cheating in colleges. (1976, June 7). *Time.* Retrieved March 21, 2006, from www.time.com.

Cheating in exams. (1967, July 12). *New York Times.* Retrieved October 21, 2006, from ProQuest Historical Newspapers.

Cheating in Florida. (1975, March 10). *Time.* Retrieved March 21, 2006, from www.time.com.

Cheating at Long Island. (1930, June 16). *Time.* Retrieved October 21, 2006, from www.time.com.

Cheating at Yale. (1930, June 16). *Time.* Retrieved October 21, 2006, from www.time.com.

Chipman, D. D., and McDonald, C. B. (1982). The cold war in the classroom: Kilpatrick's student years at Mercer. *Teacher's College Record, 83*(3), 459–465.

Christensen Hughes, J. M., and McCabe, D. L. (2006). Understanding academic misconduct. *Canadian Journal of Higher Education, 36*(1), 49–63.

Churchill, L. R. (1982). The teaching of ethics and moral values in teaching: Some contemporary conclusions. *Journal of Higher Education, 53*(3), 296–306.

Cizek, G. J. (2003). *Detecting and preventing classroom cheating: Promoting integrity in assessment.* Thousand Oaks, CA: Corwin Press.

College ousts student for plagiarism. (1965, November 22). *New York Times.* Retrieved October 21, 2006, from ProQuest Historical Newspapers.

Collison, M. N-K. (1990, January 17). Apparent rise in students' cheating worries officials: Some have brought back honor codes, started special classes. *Chronicle of Higher Education.* Retrieved October 21, 2006, from www.chronicle.com.

Columbia weighs an honor system: Students request pledges from new freshmen. (1963, September 24). *New York Times.* Retrieved October 21, 2006, from ProQuest Historical Newspapers.

Connell, C. (1981). Term paper mills continue to grind. *Educational Record, 62*(3), 19–28.

Conrad, R. (2006, March 22). University expels cheater scan. *Chronicle Herald.* Retrieved March 27, 2006, from www.ChronicleHerald.ca.

Counelis, J. S. (1993). Toward empirical studies on university ethics. *Journal of Higher Education, 64*(1), 74–92.

Covey, M. K., Saladin, S., and Killen, Pl. J. (2001). Self-monitoring, surveillance, and incentive effects on cheating. *Journal of Social Psychology, 129*(5), 673–679.

Dalton, J. C. (1998). Creating a campus climate for academic integrity. In D. D. Burnett, L. Rudolph, and K. O. Clifford (Eds.), *Academic integrity matters* (pp. 11–21). Washington, DC: National Association of Student Personnel Administrators. (ED 452 577)

Dannells, M. (1997). *From discipline to development: Rethinking student conduct in higher education.* Washington, DC: George Washington University.

Dash, N. (1960, March 13). Cheating at UCLA brings policy study: Statement being drawn to cover school principles. *Los Angeles Times.* Retrieved October 21, 2006, from ProQuest Historical Newspapers.

David, R. L., and Kovach, J. A. (1979). Attitudes towards unethical behavior as a function of educational commercialization. *College Student Journal, 13*(4), 338–344.

Davis, S. F., Grover, C. A., Becker, A. H., and McGregor, L. N. (1992). Academic dishonesty: Prevalence, determinants, techniques, and punishments. *Teaching of Psychology, 19*(1), 16–20.

Decoo, W. (2002). *Crisis on campus: Confronting academic misconduct.* Cambridge, MA: MIT Press.

DeVries, R., Anderson, M. S., and Martinson, B. C. (2006). Normal misbehavior: Scientists talk about the ethics of research. *Journal of Empirical Research on Human Research Ethics, 1*(1), 43–50.

Diekhoff, G. M., and others. (1996). College cheating: Ten years later. *Research in higher education, 37*(4), 487–502.

Donald, J. (1997). *Improving the environment for learning: Academic leaders talk about what works.* San Francisco: Jossey-Bass.

Drake, C. A. (1941). Why students cheat. *Journal of Higher Education, 12*(8), 418–420.

Drinan, P. (1999, Winter). Loyalty, learning, and academic integrity. *Liberal Education,* 28–33.

Duderstadt, J. J., Atkins, D. E., and Van Houweling, D. (2002). *Higher education in the digital age: Technology issues and strategies for American colleges and universities.* Westport, CT: Praeger.

Eble, K. E. (1977). *The craft of teaching.* San Francisco: Jossey-Bass.

Eckstein, M. A. (2003). *Combating academic fraud: Towards a culture of integrity.* Paris: International Institute for Educational Planning.

Ede, L., and Lunsford, A. A. (2001). Collaboration and concepts of authorship. *PMLA, 116*(2), 354–369.

Eighty-six cheaters punished: 2 U. of Alabama students expelled, other suspended. (1960, August 11). *New York Times.* Retrieved October 21, 2006, from ProQuest Historical Newspapers.

Eisenberg, J. (2004). To cheat or not to cheat: Effects of moral perspective and situational variables on students' attitudes. *Journal of Moral Education, 33*(2), 163–178.

El-Khawas, E. (1979). To assure fair practice toward students. *Educational Record, 60*(3), 282–294.

Evans, E. D., and Craig, D. (1990). Teacher and student perceptions of academic cheating in middle and senior high schools. *Journal of Educational Research, 84*(1), 44–52.

Evans, R., and Novak, R. (1970, May 21). The Berkeley withdrawal from academic integrity. *Los Angeles Times.* Retrieved October 21, 2006, from ProQuest Historical Newspapers.

Faia, M. (1976). How—and why—to cheat on student course evaluations. *Liberal Education, 62*(1), 113–119.

Field, K. (2007, May 15). U. of Texas at Austin fires financial-aid director implicated in student-loan scandal. *Chronicle of Higher Education.* Retrieved May 15, 2007, from www.chronicle.com.

Fifty-eight get Rutgers degrees: Dr. Metzger tells class academic integrity forbids bigotry. (1929, August 2). *New York Times.* Retrieved October 21, 2006, from ProQuest Historical Newspapers.

Fishbein, L. (1993, December 1). Curbing cheating and restoring academic integrity. *Chronicle of Higher Education.* Retrieved March 21, 2007, from www.chronicle.com.

Five in Pac-10 rules ineligible in football. (1980, August 12). *New York Times.* Retrieved October 21, 2006, from ProQuest Historical Newspapers.

Folly of plagiarism. (1901, February 23). *New York Times.* Retrieved October 21, 2006, from ProQuest Historical Newspapers.

Fox, M. F., and Braxton, J. M. (1994). Misconduct and social control in science: Issues, problems, solutions. *Journal of Higher Education, 65*(3), 373–383.

Franklyn-Stokes, A., and Newstead, S. E. (1995). Undergraduate cheating: Who does what and why? *Studies in Higher Education, 20*(2), 159–172.

Gamerman, E. (2006, January 21). Legalized "cheating." *Wall Street Journal.* Retrieved October 21, 2006, from www.wsj.com.

Gehring, D., and Pavela, G. (1994). *Issues and perceptions on academic integrity* (2nd ed.). Washington, DC: National Association of Student Personnel Administrators.

Genereux, R. L., and McLeod, B. A. (1995). Circumstances surrounding cheating: A questionnaire study of college students. *Research in Higher Education, 36*(6), 687–704.

Gerdeman, R. D. (2000). *Academic dishonesty and the community college.* Los Angeles: ERIC Clearinghouse for Community Colleges. (ED 447 840)

Giroux, H. A. (1983). Theories of reproduction and resistance in the new sociology of education: A critical analysis. *Harvard Educational Review, 53*(3), 251–293.

Goldsen, R. K., Rosenberg, M., Williams, R. M., Jr., and Suchman, E. A. (1960). *What college students think.* Princeton, NJ: Van Nostrand Company.

Goodstein, D. (1991). Scientific fraud. *American Scholar, 60*(4), 505–515.

Granitz, N., and Loewy, D. (2007). Applying ethical theories: Interpreting and responding to student plagiarism. *Journal of Business Ethics, 72,* 293–306.

Gumport, P. J., and Chun, M. (1999). Technology and higher education: Opportunities and challenges for the new era. In P. G. Altbach, R. O. Berdahl, and P. J. Gumport (Eds.), *American higher education in the twenty-first century: Social, political, and economic challenges* (pp. 370–395). Baltimore: Johns Hopkins University Press.

Guskin, A. E. (1994, September/October). Restructuring the role of faculty. *Change,* 17–25.

Haines, V. J., Diekhoff, G. M., LaBeff, E. E., and Clark, R. E. (1986). College cheating: Immaturity, lack of commitment, and the neutralizing attitude. *Research in Higher Education, 25*(4), 342–354.

Hall, T. L., and Kuh, G. D. (1998). Honor among students: Academic integrity and honor codes at state-assisted universities. *NASPA Journal, 36*(1), 2–18.

Hallak, J., and Poisson, M. (2007). *Corrupt schools, corrupt universities: What can be done?* Paris: International Institute for Educational Planning.

Hard, S. F., Conway, J. M., Moran, A. C. (2006). Faculty and colleges student beliefs about the frequency of student academic misconduct. *Journal of Higher Education, 77*(6), 1058–1080.

Hardy, R. J. (1982). Preventing academic dishonesty: Some important tips for political science professors. *Teaching Political Science, 9*(2), 68–77.

Hardy, R. J., and Burch, D. (1981). What political science professors should know in dealing with academic dishonesty. *Political Science, 9*(1), 5–14.

Hart, M., and Graham, R. (n.d.). The "new plagiarism," academic dishonesty and the development of critical thinking skills. Retrieved November 5, 2007, from www.ucw.org.uk/winbel/new_plag.doc.

Haviland, C. P., and Mullin, J. (1999). Writing centers and intellectual property. In L. Buranen and A. M. Roy (Eds.), *Perspectives on plagiarism and intellectual property in a postmodern world* (pp. 169–182). New York: State University of New York Press.

Haynes, C. C., and Berkowitz, M. W. (2007, February 20). What can schools do? *USA Today.* Retrieved November 15, 2007, from http://blogs.usatoday.com/oped/2007/02/post_48.html.

Heath, D. H. (1968). *Growing up in college: Liberal education and maturity.* San Francisco: Jossey-Bass.

Hechinger, F. M. (1965, February 7). On cheating. *New York Times.* Retrieved October 21, 2006, from ProQuest Historical Newspapers.

Hechinger, F. M. (1979, April 3). Conference dissects academic integrity. *New York Times.* Retrieved October 21, 2006, from ProQuest Historical Newspapers.

Hessinger, R. (1999). The most powerful instrument of college discipline: Student disorder and the growth of meritocracy in the colleges of the early republic. *History of Education Quarterly, 39*(3), 237–262.

Hoekema, D. A. (1990). Beyond in loco parentis? Parietal rules and moral authority. In S. M. Cahn (Ed.), *Morality, responsibility, and the university: Studies in academic ethics* (pp. 177–194). Philadelphia: Temple University Press.

Hoekema, D. A. (1994). *Campus rules and moral community: In place of in loco parentis.* Lanham, MD: Rowman & Littlefield.

Hoff, D. J. (2000, June 21). As stakes rise, definition of cheating blurs. *Educational Week.* Retrieved January 11, 2008, from www.edweek.org.

Hook, S., Kurtz, P., and Todorovich, M. (1977). *The ethics of teaching and scientific research.* Buffalo, NY: Prometheus Books.

Houston, J. P. (1976). The assessment and prevention of answer copying on undergraduate multiple-choice examinations. *Research in Higher Education, 5*(4), 301–311.

Houston, J. P. (1983). Kohlberg-type moral instruction and cheating behavior. *College Student Journal, 17*(2), 196–204.

Howard, R. M. (1995). Plagiarisms, authorships, and the academic death penalty. *College English, 57*(7), 788–806.

Howard, R. M. (2000a). The ethics of plagiarism. In M. A. Pemberton (Ed.), *The ethics of writing instruction: Issues in theory and practice* (pp. 79–90). Stamford, CT: Ablex Publishing.

Howard, R. M. (2000b). Sexuality, textuality: The cultural work of plagiarism. *College English, 62*(4), 473–491.

Howard, R. M. (2001, November 16). Forget about policing plagiarism. Just teach. *Chronicle of Higher Education.* Retrieved March 21, 2007, from www.chronicle.com.

Hutchings, P. (2002). Ethics and aspiration in the scholarship of teaching and learning. In P. A. Hutchings (Ed.), *Ethics of inquiry: Issues in the scholarship of teaching and learning* (pp. 1–17). Menlo Park, CA: Carnegie Foundation for the Advancement of Teaching.

Hutton, P. A. (2006). Understanding student cheating and what educators can do about it. *College Teaching, 54*(1), 171–176.

Introna, L., Hayes, N., Blair, L., and Wood, E. (2003). *Cultural attitudes towards plagiarism.* Lancaster, UK: Lancaster University.

Jacob, P. E. (1957). *Changing values in college.* New Haven, CT: Edward W. Hazen Foundation.

Jendrek, M. P. (1989). Faculty reactions to academic dishonesty. *Journal of College Student Development, 30*(5), 401–406.

Jesdanun, A. (2005, April 16). Experts offer free homework help online. *Associated Press.* Retrieved June 8, 2007, from www.msnbc.msn.com.

Jordan, A. E. (2001). College student cheating: The role of motivation, perceived norms, attitudes, and knowledge of institutional policy. *Ethics and Behavior, 11,* 233–247.

Kaplan, W., and Mable, P. (1998). Students' perceptions of academic integrity: Curtailing violations. In D. D. Burnett, L. Rudolph, and K. O. Clifford (Eds.), *Academic integrity matters* (pp. 22–31). Washington, DC: National Association of Student Personnel Administrators. (ED 452 577)

Karlins, M., Michaels, C., and Podlogar, S. (1988). An empirical investigation of actual cheating in a large sample of undergraduates. *Research in Higher Education, 29*(4), 359–364.

Keeling, R. P. (2004). *Learning reconsidered: A campus-wide focus on the student experience.* National Association of Student Personnel Administrators and American College Personnel Association.

Kegan, R. (1994). *In over our heads: The mental demands of modern life.* Cambridge, MA: Harvard University Press.

Keller, B. (2002, January 16). Austin cheating scandal ends in no-contest plea, fine. *Education Week.* Retrieved January 11, 2008, from www.edweek.org.

Kezar, A. J., Chambers, T. C., and Burkhardt, J. C. (2005). *Higher education for the public good: Emerging voices from a national movement.* San Francisco: Jossey-Bass.

Kibler, W. L. (1993a). Academic dishonesty: A student development dilemma. *NASPA Journal, 30*(4), 252–267.

Kibler, W. L. (1993b). A framework for addressing academic dishonesty from a student development perspective. *NASPA Journal, 31*(1), 8–18.

Kibler, W. L. (1994). Addressing academic dishonesty: What are institutions of higher education doing and not doing? *NASPA Journal, 31*(2), 92–101.

Kibler, W. L., Nuss, E. M., Paterson, B. G., and Pavela, G. (1988). *Academic integrity and student development: Legal issues and policy perspectives.* Asheville, NC: College Administration Publications.

Kilpatrick, W. H. (1925). *Foundation of method.* New York: Macmillan.

Kuehn, P., Stanwyck, D. J., and Holland, C. L. (1990). Attitudes toward "cheating" behaviors in the ESL classroom. *TESOL Quarterly, 24*(2), 313–317.

Kuh, G. D., and others. (2005). *Student success in college: Creating conditions that matter.* San Francisco: Jossey-Bass.

Lacampagne, C. B. (1993). *State of the art: Transforming ideas for teaching and learning mathematics.* (ED 360 188)

LaFollette, M. C. (1999). A foundation of trust: Scientific misconduct, congressional oversight, and the regulatory response. In J. M. Braxton (Ed.), *Perspectives on scholarly misconduct in the sciences* (pp. 11–41). Columbus: Ohio State University Press.

Lamont, L. (1979). *Campus shock: A firsthand report on college life today.* New York: E. P. Dutton.

Landis, P. H. (1954). *So this is college.* New York: McGraw-Hill.

Laney, J. T. (1990). Through thick and thin: Two ways of talking about the academy and moral responsibility. In W. M. May (Ed.), *Ethics and higher education* (pp. 49–66). New York: Macmillan.

Larkham, P. J., and Manns, S. (2002). Plagiarism and its treatment in higher education. *Journal of Further and Higher Education, 26*(4), 339–349.

Leask, B. (2006). Plagiarism, cultural diversity and metaphor: Implications for academic staff development. *Assessment and Evaluation in Higher Education, 31*(2), 183–199.

Lederman, D. (2005, November 1). Perceived plagiarism at Ohio University. *Inside Higher Education.* Retrieved May 18, 2007, from www.insidehighered.com.

Lederman, D. (2006, November 9). Southern Illinois chancellor forced out. *Inside Higher Education.* Retrieved November 9, 2006, from www.insidehighered.com.

Lederman, D., and Redden, E. (2007, January 31). Accountability and comparability. *Inside Higher Education.* Retrieved January 31, 2007, from www.insidehighered.com.

Levy, E. S., and Rakovski, C. C. (2006). Academic dishonesty: A zero tolerance professor and student registration choices. *Research in Higher Education, 47*(6), 735–754.

Lewis, K. H., and Hartnett, J. J. (1983). *Sex differences in the perception of male/female unethical behavior.* Paper presented at the annual meeting of the Southeastern Psychological Association, March 23–26, Atlanta, GA. (ED 234 316)

Lin, C-H. S., and Wen, L-Y. M. (2006). Academic dishonesty in higher education: A nationwide study in Taiwan. *Higher Education, 54*(1), 85–97.

Lindey, A. (1952). *Plagiarism and originality.* New York: Harper & Brothers.

Loofbourow, G. C., and Keys, N. (1933). A group test of problem behavior tendencies in junior high school boys. *Journal of Educational Psychology, 24*(9), 641–653.

Louis, K. S., Anderson, M. S., and Rosenberg, L. (1995). Academic misconduct and values: The department's influence. *Review of Higher Education, 18*(4), 393–422.

Lucas, C. J. (1994). *American higher education: A history.* New York: St. Martin's Griffin.

Magolda, M.B.B. (1999). *Creating contexts for learning and self-authorship: Constructive-developmental pedagogy.* Nashville: Vanderbilt University Press.

Malcolm, J., and Ng, S. H. (2001). Relationship of self-awareness to cheating on an external standard of competence. *Journal of Social Psychology, 129*(3), 391–395.

Malinowski, C. I., and Smith, C. (1985). Moral reasoning and moral conduct: An investigation prompted by Kohlberg's theory. *Journal of Personality and Social Psychology, 49,* 1016–1027.

Maller, J. B. (1932). The measurement of conflict between honesty and group loyalty. *Journal of Educational Psychology, 23*(3), 187–191.

Marcoux, H. E. (2001). Development and integrity course syllabus. Kansas State University. Retrieved February 10, 2007, from www.k-state.edu/honor/aiclass/syllabuss06.htm.

Markie, P. J. (1994). *A professor's duties: Ethical issues in college teaching.* Lanham, MD: Rowan & Littlefield.

Marsh, W. C. (2004). *Knowledge incorporated: Plagiarism and anti-plagiarism therapies in higher education.* Doctoral dissertation, University of California, San Diego.

Maruca, L. (2001). Plagiarism. In L. Becker (Ed.), *Encyclopedia of Ethics* (Vol. 3, pp. 1126–1130). New York: Routledge.

Maruca, L. (2003). Plagiarism and its (disciplinary) discontents: Towards an interdisciplinary theory and pedagogy. *Issues in Integrative Studies, 21,* 74–97.

Maruca, L. (2005). The plagiarism panic: Digital policing in the new intellectual property regime. In F. MacMillan (Ed.), *New Directions in Copyright Law,* (2, pp. 241–261). London: Edward Elgar Publishing.

Matthews, C. O. (1932). The honor system. *Journal of Higher Education, 3*(8), 411–415.

Mawdsley, R. D. (1994). *Academic misconduct: Cheating and plagiarism.* Topeka, KS: National Organization on Legal Problems of Education.

McBee, M. L. (1978). Higher education: Its responsibility for moral development. *Phi Kappa Phi Journal, 58*(2), 30–33.

McCabe, D. L. (1992). The influence of situational ethics on cheating among college students. *Sociological Inquiry, 62*(3), 365–374.

McCabe, D. L. (1993). Faculty responses to academic dishonesty: The influence of honor codes. *Research in Higher Education, 34*(5), 647–658.

McCabe, D. L. (2005a). Cheating among college and university students: A North American perspective. *International Journal of Educational Integrity, 1*(1), 1–11.

McCabe, D. L. (2005b, Summer/Fall). It takes a village: Academic dishonesty and educational opportunity. *Liberal Education,* 26–31.

McCabe, D. L., and Bowers, W. J. (1994, January). Academic dishonesty among males in college: A thirty-year perspective. *Journal of College Student Development, 35,* 5–10.

McCabe, D. L., and Drinan, P. (1999, October 15). Toward a culture of academic integrity. *Chronicle of Higher Education.* Retrieved November 2, 2002, from www.chronicle.com.

McCabe, D. L., and Pavela, G. (n.d.) The effect of institutional policies and procedures on academic integrity. Unpublished manuscript.

McCabe, D. L., and Pavela, G. (2000, September/October). Some good news about academic integrity. *Change,* 32–38.

McCabe, D. L., and Trevino, L. K. (1993). Academic dishonesty: Honor codes and other contextual influences. *Journal of Higher Education, 64*(5), 522–538.

McCabe, D. L., and Trevino, L. K. (1996, January/February). What we know about cheating in college: Longitudinal trends and recent developments. *Change,* 29–33.

McCabe, D. L., and Trevino, L. K. (1997). Individual and contextual influences on academic dishonesty: A multicampus investigation. *Research in Higher Education, 38*(3), 379–396.

McCabe, D. L., and Trevino, L. K. (2002). Honesty and honor codes. *Academe, 88*(1), 37–41.

McCabe, D. L., Trevino, L. K., and Butterfield, K. D. (1999). Academic integrity in honor code and non–honor code environments. *Journal of Higher Education, 70*(2), 211–233.

McCabe, D. L., Trevino, L. K., and Butterfield, K. D. (2001). Cheating in academic institutions: A decade of research. *Ethics and Behavior, 11*(3), 219–233.

McFall, L. (1987). Integrity. *Ethics, 98*(1), 5–20.

McGrath, E. (1982, May 31). Questioning campus discipline. *Time.* Retrieved March 21, 2006, from www.time.com.

McKenzie, R. B. (1979a). Cheating and chiseling. In R. B. McKenzie (Ed.), *The political economy of the educational process* (pp. 173–188). Boston: Martinus Nijhoff Publishing.

McKenzie, R. B. (1979b). An introduction to the economics of education. In R. B. McKenzie (Ed.), *The political economy of the educational process* (pp. 1–12). Boston: Martinus Nijhoff Publishing.

McLaren, P. (1989). *Life in schools: An introduction to critical pedagogy in the foundations of education.* New York: Longman.

McLeod, S. H. (1992). Responding to plagiarism: The role of the WPA. *Writing Program Administration, 15*(3), 7–16.

Michaels, J. W., and Miethe, T. D. (1989). Applying theories of deviance to academic cheating, *Social Science Quarterly, 70*(4), 870–885.

Middlebrook, S. (1961, April 9). No panacea for college cheating. *New York Times.* Retrieved October 21, 2006, from ProQuest Historical Newspapers.

Monastersky, R. (2006, November 29). Science journals must develop stronger safeguards against fraud, panel says. *Chronicle of Higher Education* Retrieved November 29, 2006, from www.chronicle.com.

Moore, K. M. (1978). The war with the tutors: Student-faculty conflict at Harvard and Yale, 1745–1771. *History of Education Quarterly, 18*(2), 115–127.

Morrison, P. (1976, July 11). Student cheaters: They crave success. *Los Angeles Times.* Retrieved October 21, 2006, from ProQuest Historical Newspapers.

Muelder, W. G. (1978). Empowerment and the integrity of higher education. In D. B. Robertson (Ed.), *Power and empowerment in higher education* (pp. 1–20). Lexington: University Press of Kentucky.

Murphy, R. (1990). Anorexia: The cheating disorder. *College English, 52*(8), 898–903.

Oblinger, D. G., and Rush, S. C. (1997). The learning revolution. In D. G. Oblinger and S. C. Rush (Eds.), *The learning revolution: The challenge of information technology in the academy* (pp. 2–19). Bolton, MA: Anker Publishing Company.

Pace, R. F. (2004). *Halls of honor: College men in the old south.* Baton Rouge: Louisiana State University Press.

Paine, L. S. (1994). Managing for organizational integrity. *Harvard Business Review, 72*(2), 106–117.

Palmer, P. J. (1998). *The courage to teach: Exploring the inner landscape of a teacher's life.* San Francisco: Jossey-Bass.

Park, C. (2003). In other (people's) words: Plagiarism by university students—literature and lessons. *Assessment and Evaluation in Higher Education, 28*(5), 471–488.

Park, C. (2004). Rebels without a clause: Towards an institutional framework for dealing with plagiarism by students. *Journal of Further and Higher Education, 28*(3), 291–306.

Parr, F. W. (1936). The problem of student honesty. *Journal of Higher Education, 7*(6), 318–326.

Passow, H. J., and others. (2006). Factors influencing engineering students' decisions to cheat by type of assessment. *Research in Higher Education, 47*(6), 643–684.

Payne, S. L., and Nantz, K. S. (1994). Social accounts and metaphors about cheating. *College Teaching, 42,* 90–96.

Pollard, W. B. (1972, June 17). 600 students face action for buying their term papers. *Los Angeles Times.* Retrieved October 21, 2006, from ProQuest Historical Newspapers.

Pratt, C. B., and McLaughlin, G. W. (1989). An analysis of predictors of college students' ethical inclinations. *Research in Higher Education, 30*(2), 195–219.

Puka, B. (2005, Summer/Fall). Student cheating. *Liberal Education, 32*–35.

Pulvers, K., and Diekhoff, G. M. (1999). The relationship between academic dishonesty and college classroom environment. *Research in Higher Education, 40*(4), 487–498.

Pusey, N. M. (1978). *American higher education, 1945–1970: A personal report.* Cambridge, MA: Harvard University Press.

Rafferty, M. (1965, June 7). Cheaters eventually flunk life. *Los Angeles Times.* Retrieved October 21, 2006, from ProQuest Historical Newspapers.

Ray, D. (2006). A million little pieces of shame (editorial). *Plagiary,* 1. Retrieved online March 21, 2006, from www.plagiary.org.

Rentz, A. L. (1996). A history of student affairs. In A. L. Rentz (Ed.), *Student affairs practice in higher education* (2nd Ed., pp. 28–55). Springfield, IL: Charles C. Thomas.

Rhoades, L. J. (2004). New institutional research misconduct activity: 1992–2001. Retrieved November 26, 2007, from http://ori.dhhs.gov/misconduct/documents.

Rich, J. M. (1984). *Professional ethics in education.* Springfield, IL: Charles C. Thomas.

Roark, A. C. (1981, July 30). Out of hand? Cheating: A campus problem. *Los Angeles Times*. Retrieved October 21, 2006, from ProQuest Historical Newspapers.

Roberts, D., and Rabinowitz, W. (1992). An investigation of student perceptions of cheating in academic situations. *Review of Higher Education, 15*(2), 179–190.

Robinson-Zañartu, C., and others. (2005). Academic crime and punishment: Faculty members' perceptions of and responses to plagiarism. *School Psychology Quarterly, 20*(3), 318–337.

Roig, M. (2001). Plagiarism and paraphrasing criteria of college and university professors. *Ethics and Behaviors, 11*(3), 307–323.

Ronning, E. A., Anderson, M. S., de Vries, R., and Martinson, B. C. (2007). *Testing ethical borderlines: Bending the rules of science.* Paper presented at the annual meeting of the American Education Research Association. April. Louisville, KY.

Rudolph, L., and Timm, L. (1998). A comprehensive approach for creating a campus climate that promotes academic integrity. In D. D. Burnett, L. Rudolph, and K. O. Clifford (Eds.), *Academic integrity matters* (pp. 64–82). Washington, DC: National Association of Student Personnel Administrators. (ED 452 577)

Schemo, D. J. (2001, May 10). U. of Virginia hit by scandal over cheating. *New York Times*. Retrieved October 21, 2006, from ProQuest Historical Newspapers.

Schnepp, A. F. (1940). College students' principles of honesty. *Journal of Higher Education, 11*(2), 81–84.

Schroeder, C. C. (1996, Fall). Partnerships: An imperative for enhancing student learning and institutional effectiveness. *New Directions for Student Services, 87*, 5–18.

Schurr, G. M. (1982). Toward a code of ethics for academics. *Journal of Higher Education, 53*(3), 318–334.

Scriven, M. (1982). Professorial ethics. *Journal of Higher Education, 53*(3), 307–317.

Seriup Pincus, H., and Pedhazur Schmelkin, L. (2003). Faculty perceptions of academic dishonesty: A multidimensional scaling analysis. *Journal of Higher Education, 74*(2), 196–209.

Setran, D. P. (2005). From moral aristocracy to Christian social democracy: The transformation of character education in the Hi-Y, 1910–1940. *History of Education Quarterly, 45*(2), 207–246.

Sewall, G., and Drake, S. (1980, May 26). An epidemic of cheating. *Newsweek*. Retrieved March 21, 2006, from LexisNexis.

Shaffer, H. B. (1966, May 11). Cheating in school. *Editorial Research Reports, 1*, 343–358.

Shils, E. (1978, Spring). The academic ethos. *American Scholar, 47*, 165–190.

Shils, E. (1983). *The academic ethic.* Chicago: University of Chicago Press.

Shurtleff, R. F. (1968). Plagiarism: The gray area. In C. W. Havice (Ed.), *Campus values* (pp. 88–94). New York: Charles Scribner's Sons.

Simmons, S. C. (1999). Competing notions of authorship: A historical look at students and textbooks on plagiarism and cheating. In L. Buranen and A. M. Roy (Eds.), *Perspectives on plagiarism and intellectual property in a postmodern world* (pp. 41–54). New York: State University of New York Press.

Sims, R. L. (1993). The relationship between academic dishonesty and unethical business practices. *Journal of Education for Business, 68*(4), 207–211.

Slaughter, S., and Leslie, L. L. (1997). *Academic capitalism: Politics, policies, and the entrepreneurial university.* Baltimore: Johns Hopkins University Press.

Slaughter, S., and Rhoades, G. (2004). *Academic capitalism and the new economy: Markets, state, and higher education.* Baltimore: Johns Hopkins University Press.

Smith, D. C., and Reynolds, C. H. (1990). Institutional culture and ethics. In W. M. May (Ed.), *Ethics and higher education* (pp. 21–31). New York: Macmillan.

Sowden, C. (2004). Plagiarism and the culture of multilingual students in higher education abroad. *ELT Journal, 59*(3), 226–233.

Stanwyck, D. J., and Abdelal, P. (1984). *Attitudes toward cheating behavior in the ESL classroom.* Paper presented at a meeting of the Eastern Educational Research Association, February, West Palm Beach, FL. (ED 250 927)

Starratt, R. J. (1994). *Building an ethical school: A practical response to the moral crisis in schools.* London: Falmer Press.

Stearns, S. A. (2001). The student-instructor relationship's effect on academic integrity. *Ethics and Behavior, 11*(3), 275–285.

Steininger, M., Johnson, R. E., and Kirts, D. K. (1964). Cheating on college examinations as a function of situationally aroused anxiety and hostility. *Journal of Educational Psychology, 55*(6), 317–324.

Steneck, N. (1992, March). University and government approaches to fostering research integrity. *University of Minnesota Research Review, 6,* 19–20.

Stiggins, R. J. (2002). Assessment crisis: The absence of assessment *for* learning. *Phi Delta Kappan, 83*(10), 758–765.

Students find college honor codes losing favor. (1975, April 12). *New York Times.* Retrieved October 21, 2006, from ProQuest Historical Newspapers.

Su, E. Y., and Magee, M. (2007, December 12). Audit turns acclaim into outrage at Preuss. *Union-Tribune.* Retrieved December 19, 2007, from signonsandiego.com.

Swartz, P. C., Carlisle, B. A., and Uyeki, E. C. (2007). Libraries and student affairs: Partners for student success. *Reference Services Review, 35*(1), 109–122.

Tapscott, D. (1998). *Growing up digital: The rise of the net generation.* New York: McGraw-Hill.

Thelin, J. R. (2004). *A history of American higher education.* Baltimore: Johns Hopkins University Press.

Tierney, W. (1991). Ideology and identity in higher institutions. In W. G. Tierney (Ed.), *Culture and ideology in higher education: Advancing a critical agenda* (pp. 35–58). New York: Praeger.

Tolchin, M. (1965, November 22). Cheating rising in city schools. *New York Times.* Retrieved October 21, 2006, from ProQuest Historical Newspapers.

Townley, C., and Parsell, M. (2004). Technology and academic virtue: Student plagiarism through the looking glass. *Ethics and Information Technology, 6,* 271–277.

Trachtenberg, S. J. (1972). What happened to the buffalo? *Change, 4*(8), 45–47.

Trombley, W. (1965, February 7). Exam honor code called failure by UCLA dean. *Los Angeles Times.* Retrieved October 21, 2006, from ProQuest Historical Newspapers.

Tucker, D. L. (2003). *Understanding learning styles and study strategies of Korean students in American colleges and universities.* (ED 478 616)

Turiel, E. (1983). *The development of social knowledge: Morality and convention.* Cambridge: Cambridge University Press.

University of California, Santa Barbara (2005). Student conduct and discipline. *Campus Regulations* (Chapter 7). Retrieved February 8, 2007, from www.ucsb.edu.

University Fraud. (2007, February 12). *Maclean's Magazine.* Retrieved June 12, 2007, from www.macleans.ca.

University of Maryland. (2005). Code of academic integrity. Retrieved May 21, 2007, from http://www.studenthonorcouncil.umd.edu/code.html.

Vaidhyanathan, S. (2001). *Copyrights and copywrongs: The rise of intellectual property and how it threatens creativity.* New York: New York University Press.

Vaidhyanathan, S. (2004). *The anarchist in the library: How the clash between freedom and control is hacking the real world and crashing the system.* New York: Basic Books.

Valentine, K. (2006). Plagiarism as literacy practice: Recognizing and rethinking ethical binaries. *College Composition and Communication, 58*(1), 89–109.

Wagoner, J. L., Jr. (1986). Honor and dishonor at Mr. Jefferson's university: The antebellum years. *History of Education Quarterly, 26*(2), 155–179.

Wagoner, W. D. (1968). The campus and the generation gap. In C. W. Havice (Ed.), *Campus values* (pp. 17–23). New York: Charles Scribner's Sons.

Ward, D. A. (2001). Self-esteem and dishonest behavior revisited. *The Journal of Social Psychology, 126*(6), 709–713.

Ward, K. (2003). *Faculty service roles and the scholarship of engagement.* San Francisco: Jossey-Bass.

Weber, L. J., McBee, J. K., and Krebs, J. E. (1983). Take home tests: An experimental study. *Research in Higher Education, 18*(2), 473–483.

Wentworth, E. (1976, May 7). Forgers and imposters worry colleges: Hard-to-enter law and medical schools often victims. *Los Angeles Times.* Retrieved October 21, 2006, from ProQuest Historical Newspapers.

Western Association of Schools and Colleges. (2001). *Initial visits procedure manual.* Retrieved November 15, 2007, from http://www.acswasc.org/pdf_fol/FOL_Initial_visit_procedures.pdf.

What price honor? (1976, June 7). *Time.* Retrieved October 21, 2006, from ProQuest Historical Newspapers.

Whicker, M. L., and Kronenfeld, J. J. (1994). *Dealing with ethical dilemmas on campus.* Thousand Oaks, CA: Sage Publications.

Whitley, B. E., Jr., and Keith-Spiegel, P. (2001). Academic integrity as an institutional issue. *Ethics and Behavior, 11*(3), 325–342.

Whitley, B. E., Jr., and Keith-Spiegel, P. (2002). *Academic dishonesty: An educator's guide.* Mahwah, NJ: Erlbaum.

Wilcox, J. R., and Ebbs, S. L. (1992). *The leadership compass: Values and ethics in higher education.* Report No. EDO-HE-92-1. Washington, DC: ERIC Clearinghouse on Higher Education. (ED 350 970)

William and Mary Student Handbook. (2007–2008). Background of the honor system. Retrieved November 12, 2007, from www.mw.edu/deanofstudents/judicial/ honorhistory.php.

Wilson, E. K. (1982). Power, pretense, and piggybacking: Some ethical issues in teaching. *Journal of Higher Education, 53*(3), 268–281.

Wilson, M. E. (2004, Summer). Teaching, learning, and millennial students. *New Directions for Student Services, 106,* 59–71.

Wilson, R. (1999, October 15). Colleges urged to better define academic integrity and to stress its importance. *Chronicle of Higher Education.* Retrieved June 28, 2006, from www.chronicle.com.

Wilson, W. (1905, August 12). The honor system in school and college. *New York Times.* Retrieved October 21, 2006, from ProQuest Historical Newspapers.

Young, J. R. (2007, April 30). Cheating incident involving 34 students at Duke is business school's biggest ever. *Chronicle of Higher Education.* Retrieved April 30, 2007, from www.chronicle.com.

Young, R. B. (1997). *No neutral ground: Standing by the values we prize in higher education.* San Francisco: Jossey-Bass.

Zelna, C. L., and Bresciani, M. J. (2004). Assessing and addressing academic integrity at a doctoral extensive institution. *NASPA Journal, 42*(1), 72–93.

Name Index

A

Aaron, R. M., 30, 110
Ajzen, I., 51, 52, 56
Akst, D., 24
Allmendinger, D. F., Jr., 14, 15
Alschuler, A. S., 49, 52, 71, 109
Amsden, D., 21, 49, 54, 56
Anderson, M. S., 3, 11, 26, 99
Angell, R. C., 17–18, 20, 45, 48, 51, 76
Anglen, R., 2, 26
Appel-Silbaugh, C. D., 112
Apple, M., 49, 57
Appleton, J., 90, 93, 94
Armentrout, W. D., 84
Arnstine, D., 70, 92
Astin, A., 5, 6, 73, 88
Atkins, D. E., 69, 70, 83

B

Baird, J. S., Jr., 8
Barnes, W. F., 49, 54
Barnett, D. C., 5, 8, 54, 75
Barr, R. B., 69, 88, 109
Bass, R., 66
Batson, T., 66
Bayer, A. E., 26, 30, 53, 97
Beck, L., 51, 52, 56
Becker, A. H., 49, 50, 52
Becker, H. S., 22, 53, 55
Beckham, J. C., 37, 97
Bellico, R., 54

Berkowitz, M. W., 2
Bertram Gallant, T., 4, 25, 30, 54, 57, 59, 66, 70, 71, 73, 110
Besvinick, S. L., 73
Blair, L., 54, 75, 81, 91, 94
Blimling, G. S., 49, 52, 71, 109
Blizek, W. L., 73
Boice, B., 53
Bok, D., 5, 48, 54, 60, 73
Bowden, D., 75, 80
Bowers, W. J., 29, 45, 55
Bowman, J., 19, 31
Boynton, R. S., 2, 69
Braxton, J. M., 3, 26, 30, 53, 97
Bray, N. J., 97
Briggs, L.B.R., 18, 19, 48, 51
Brimble, M., 3, 8, 51, 68, 84
Brown, V. J., 68, 108
Bruffee, K. A., 69, 81, 84, 90, 91, 100
Bruster, B., 68
Buchanan, J. H., 37, 97
Bunn, D. N., 49, 54
Burch, D., 38
Burkhardt, J. C., 5
Burrus, R. T., 9, 29
Bush, D. K., 27, 38, 45, 110
Butterfield, K. D., 31, 76

C

Callahan, D., 2, 3, 8, 13, 51, 72
Cardill, S. B., 49

Tolchin, M., 24
Townley, C., 5, 25, 54, 68, 77, 83, 90, 91
Trachtenberg, S. J., 21, 22
Trevino, L. K., 1, 3, 8, 13, 31, 45, 52, 53, 72, 76
Trombley, W., 45
Tucker, D. L., 75
Turiel, E., 75

V

Vaidhyanathan, S., 58, 66, 67, 68, 83
Valentine, K., 9, 59
Van Houweling, D., 69, 70, 83

W

Wagoner, W. D., 15, 16, 65
Ward, D. A., 16, 50, 51

Ward, K., 13, 20, 25
Weber, L. J., 8
Wentworth, E., 25
Whicker, M. L., 5, 98
Whitley, B. E., Jr., 5, 34, 49, 52, 71, 72, 88, 89, 92, 93, 113
Wilcox, J. R., 49, 52
Williams, R. M., Jr., 52
Wilson, E. K., 53, 54
Wilson, M. E., 68
Wilson, R., 27
Wilson, W., 19
Wood, E., 54, 75, 81, 91, 94

Y

Young, J. R., 66
Young, R. B., 85

Subject Index

Antellum colleges (1760–1860)
approaches to academic misconduct by, 15–16
description of, 14
misconduct defined by, 14–15
Arnstine, D., 70
Assessment
academic integrity link to, 94–95
benefits of using learning, 95
of your organizational strategy, 106
Association of American Colleges and Universities, 5, 6, 88, 90
Authorship
plagiarism tied to notion of, 57–58
policies acknowledging conflicts of information, knowledge and, 99–100
technology as redefining concept of, 66–67. *See also* Originality notion

B

The Boston Globe expos['] (1971), 21

C

CAI (Center for Academic Integrity), 1, 38, 45
"California idea" of education, 16–17
Campus climate/culture
classroom dynamics and, 53–54
described, 51–52
peer norms and, 52–53
Campus Shock (Lamont), 25
Carnegie Council report (1979), 26
Center for Academic Integrity, 1, 38, 45
The Cheating Culture (Callahan), 8, 13
Classroom dynamics, 53–54
"Classroom incivilities," 53
Clemson University, 1
Collaboration
cultural differences regarding, 75–76
inconsistencies regarding policies on, 93–94
Napster-like sharing changing definition of, 58–59, 69–70
notion of "unauthorized," 84–85

Columbia University, 23
Columbia Weighs an Honor System (1963), 1
Commission on Academic Integrity (Columbia College), 23
Copyright Act (1909), 16
"Cribbing," 18
Critical theory, 57–59
Cultural differences, 75–76

D

Diversification, 74–77, 78
Duke University, 66

E

Education Act (Britain, 1988), 56

F

Fabrication, 10
Faculty
connections between misconduct of students and, 110–111
critical theory on societal factors affecting, 57–59
empowering student academic development, 84–85
factors affecting teacher role of, 81
game of war between students and, 17–18
learning-oriented environment creating by, 89–90
rule-compliance strategy and policeman role of, 81. *See also* Teaching
Faculty-student relationships
critical theory on societal factors affecting, 57–59
effects on conduct by, 30
empowering student academic development through, 84–85
impact on teacher role of faculty, 81
strains and tensions inherent in, 79–81. *See also* Students
Falsification, 10
Free Speech
How to Express Your Message (UCSD), 37

About the Author

Tricia Bertram Gallant is the academic integrity coordinator for the University of California, San Diego. She earned her Ph.D. in leadership with a focus on higher education from the University of San Diego. She previously served as a director on the board of the Center for Academic Integrity and more recently serves on its advisory council. Bertram Gallant has also been active in the classroom, teaching leadership and higher education administration to undergraduates and graduates. Her work on academic integrity and leadership has appeared in edited books and journals, including the *Journal of Higher Education, Review of Higher Education,* and *NASPA.*

About the ASHE Higher Education Report Series

Since 1983, the ASHE (formerly ASHE-ERIC) Higher Education Report Series has been providing researchers, scholars, and practitioners with timely and substantive information on the critical issues facing higher education. Each monograph presents a definitive analysis of a higher education problem or issue, based on a thorough synthesis of significant literature and institutional experiences. Topics range from planning to diversity and multiculturalism, to performance indicators, to curricular innovations. The mission of the Series is to link the best of higher education research and practice to inform decision making and policy. The reports connect conventional wisdom with research and are designed to help busy individuals keep up with the higher education literature. Authors are scholars and practitioners in the academic community. Each report includes an executive summary, review of the pertinent literature, descriptions of effective educational practices, and a summary of key issues to keep in mind to improve educational policies and practice.

The Series is one of the most peer reviewed in higher education. A National Advisory Board made up of ASHE members reviews proposals. A National Review Board of ASHE scholars and practitioners reviews completed manuscripts. Six monographs are published each year and they are approximately 120 pages in length. The reports are widely disseminated through Jossey-Bass and John Wiley & Sons, and they are available online to subscribing institutions through Wiley InterScience (http://www.interscience.wiley.com).

Call for Proposals

The ASHE Higher Education Report Series is actively looking for proposals. We encourage you to contact one of the editors, Dr. Kelly Ward (kaward@wsu.edu) or Dr. Lisa Wolf-Wendel (lwolf@ku.edu), with your ideas.

Recent Titles

ASHE HIGHER EDUCATION REPORT
Order Form
SUBSCRIPTIONS AND SINGLE ISSUES

DISCOUNTED BACK ISSUES:

*Use this form to receive **20% off** all back issues of ASHE Higher Education Report. All single issues priced at **$22.40** (normally $28.00)*

TITLE	ISSUE NO.	ISBN

Call 888-378-2537 *or see mailing instructions below. When calling, mention the promotional code, JB7ND, to receive your discount.*

SUBSCRIPTIONS: *(1 year, 6 issues)*

☐ New Order   ☐ Renewal

U.S.	☐ Individual: $165	☐ Institutional: $199
Canada/Mexico	☐ Individual: $165	☐ Institutional: $235
All Others	☐ Individual: $201	☐ Institutional: $310

Call 888-378-2537 *or see mailing and pricing instructions below. Online subscriptions are available at www.interscience.wiley.com.*

Copy or detach page and send to:
John Wiley & Sons, Journals Dept., 5th Floor
989 Market Street, San Francisco, CA 94103-1741

Order Form can also be faxed to: 888-481-2665

Issue/Subscription Amount: $ _____	**SHIPPING CHARGES:**	
Shipping Amount: $ _____	SURFACE	Domestic Canadian
(for single issues only—subscription prices include shipping)	First Item	$5.00 $6.00
Total Amount: $ _____	Each Add'l Item	$3.00 $1.50

(No sales tax for U.S. subscriptions. Canadian residents, add GST for subscription orders. Individual rate subscriptions must be paid by personal check or credit card. Individual rate subscriptions may not be resold as library copies.)

☐ Payment enclosed (U.S. check or money order only. All payments must be in U.S. dollars.)

☐ VISA ☐ MC ☐ Amex # _____ Exp. Date _____

Card Holder Name _____ Card Issue # _____

Signature _____ Day Phone _____

☐ Bill Me (U.S. institutional orders only. Purchase order required.)

Purchase order # _____
Federal Tax ID13559302   GST 89102 8052

Name _____

Address _____

Phone _____ E-mail _____

JB7ND

**ASHE-ERIC HIGHER EDUCATION REPORT
IS NOW AVAILABLE ONLINE AT WILEY INTERSCIENCE**

What is Wiley InterScience?

Wiley InterScience is the dynamic online content service from John Wiley & Sons delivering the full text of over 300 leading scientific, technical, medical, and professional journals, plus major reference works, the acclaimed Current Protocols laboratory manuals, and even the full text of select Wiley print books online.

What are some special features of Wiley InterScience?

Wiley Interscience Alerts is a service that delivers table of contents via e-mail for any journal available on Wiley InterScience as soon as a new issue is published online.
Early View is Wiley's exclusive service presenting individual articles online as soon as they are ready, even before the release of the compiled print issue. These articles are complete, peer-reviewed, and citable.
CrossRef is the innovative multi-publisher reference linking system enabling readers to move seamlessly from a reference in a journal article to the cited publication, typically located on a different server and published by a different publisher.

How can I access Wiley InterScience?

Visit http://www.interscience.wiley.com.

Guest Users can browse Wiley InterScience for unrestricted access to journal Tables of Contents and Article Abstracts, or use the powerful search engine.
Registered Users are provided with a *Personal Home Page* to store and manage customized alerts, searches, and links to favorite journals and articles. Additionally, Registered Users can view free Online Sample Issues and preview selected material from major reference works.
Licensed Customers are entitled to access full-text journal articles in PDF, with select journals also offering full-text HTML.

How do I become an Authorized User?

Authorized Users are individuals authorized by a paying Customer to have access to the journals in Wiley InterScience. For example, a University that subscribes to Wiley journals is considered to be the Customer.

Faculty, staff and students authorized by the University to have access to those journals in Wiley InterScience are Authorized Users. Users should contact their Library for information on which Wiley journals they have access to in Wiley InterScience.

ASK YOUR INSTITUTION ABOUT WILEY INTERSCIENCE TODAY!